THE
POCKET
IDIOT'S
GUIDE™ TO

Mortgages

by Edie Milligan and
Jamie Sutton

ALPHA

A member of Penguin Group (USA) Inc.

To my mother, Suzanne Milligan, who defined for me how you
make a house into a home.
—Edie Milligan

To my husband, Gerald Sutton, my soul mate.
—Jamie Sutton

Copyright © 2003 by Edie Milligan and Jamie Sutton

International Standard Book Number: 1-59257-125-5
Library of Congress Catalog Card Number: 2003106942

05   04   8   7   6   5   4   3   2

Interpretation of the printing code: The rightmost number of the first
series of numbers is the year of the book's printing; the rightmost number of the second series of numbers is the number of the book's printing.
For example, a printing code of 03-1 shows that the first printing
occurred in 2003.

Printed in the United States of America

Note: This publication contains the opinions and ideas of its authors. It
is intended to provide helpful and informative material on the subject
matter covered. It is sold with the understanding that the authors and
publisher are not engaged in rendering professional services in the book.
If the reader requires personal assistance or advice, a competent professional should be consulted.

The authors and publisher specifically disclaim any responsibility for
any liability, loss, or risk, personal or otherwise, which is incurred as a
consequence, directly or indirectly, of the use and application of any of
the contents of this book.

Most Alpha books are available at special quantity discounts for bulk purchases for sales promotions, premiums, fund-raising, or educational use.
Special books, or book excerpts, can also be created to fit specific needs.

For details, write: Special Markets, Alpha Books, 375 Hudson Street,
New York, NY 10014.

Contents

Introduction

Buying a home is exciting, because a home is more than just a house or condo that you live in. It's not just a roof over your head. It's a symbol of success and stability in this culture. When you buy a home, you have, in a sense, graduated financially. You've accumulated savings that you will convert into another type of asset. You've withstood the scrutiny of a lender and passed their tests on income and credit. You have shown others and yourself that you are worthy of purchasing your home, which over time may store a significant chunk of your financial net worth as well.

Because your home plays such an important part in your life, it's worth taking the time to educate yourself on how to make the purchase a good financial decision as well as the wonderful, emotionally charged purchase that it is.

As you read through this book, my hope is that I've anticipated most of your questions and offered solutions that help you to become more confident in the loan process. The word *process* means an ongoing action. Not everyone who reads this book will be ready to purchase and finance a home tomorrow. You can be assured, though, that with a little advance planning, any circumstance that presently stands in your way can be easily overcome. And the resulting home purchase will be a better, more pleasant experience for your advance efforts.

Acknowledgments

As two self-employed moms, our husbands and kids are used to us meeting deadlines and attending to the needs of our clients. Jerry, Paul, Will, Audrey, Eric, and Lydia were truly wonderful as they shared their time so we could write this valuable guide for families everywhere.

We'd like to thank Mike Sanders and his team at Alpha for guiding us through the magical process of publishing. Even though this is a short book, it was given the same attention and professional care that every book deserves.

Several colleagues were invaluable as pieces of the book came together. Thank you to Eric Westerhausen for his thoughts, wisdom, and insight. And we'd like to thank Todd Kerr, Brian Kemp, Anita Padilla, Barbara Funke, Will Rogers, Barry Yaillen, Jill Gianola, Michael Schulman, Mike Moss and his fabulous staff at Northwest Title, and Cara, Danielle, and Robin, for helping us research, review, and revise our work.

Trademarks

Chapter 1

Before You Start Looking at Homes

In This Chapter

- Figuring out what you can afford
- Understanding the difference between affording and qualifying
- Budgeting for expenses

There is something magical about owning your own home. There must be, because otherwise why would you eagerly ask for plumbing bills, leaky roofs, and increasing tax bills? The security, sense of stability, and connection to community that comes from being a homeowner is priceless to some. Unfortunately, this quest for intangible benefits leaves some home shoppers ignoring the financial realities of homeownership.

So before you look at even one house, you have some thinking and calculating to do. Only then can you set out on the most exciting shopping trip of your life, with the confidence that you are making the right decisions based on the best information.

If you find your dream home first, fall in love with the neighborhood, and start redecorating it in your mind, you might allow yourself to feel pressured by mortgage companies to accept terms and jump through unnecessary hoops. Keep yourself in the driver's seat by resolving all the purely business decisions before you cross over into the dream state of home shopping.

How Much Home Can You Afford?

As you begin to look at a home purchase, the first question that typically comes to mind is "How much home can I afford?" The answer to this question requires some careful thought and planning. The sales price, loan product, and monies available to put toward the purchase all play a role in the final purchase amount, so let's start with how to choose a price range of homes to look for.

There are two (sometimes very different) answers to the "How much home can I afford?" question. The lending institution you choose (see Chapter 2) will determine a number and you will have to determine a number (later in the chapter). Both must be explored before coming up with the *final answer*.

The good news is, there may be a tax benefit for ownership. The federal government will allow you to use the interest paid each month, along with the property taxes you've paid in the filing year, as an itemized deduction against taxable income. Note at this point, though, that because you'll have a tax benefit never realized before, it's like getting a raise, without asking for it, monthly.

This "raise" needs to be taken for what it is, however. Lenders use qualification calculations developed over time to guide you in your home buying; they've taken into account that there's more money in your household budget due to the tax benefit. So when they say that you can afford more than what you've paid in rent in the past, keep that in mind. If you are purchasing a lower-priced home during a low interest rate cycle, you may not see a tax benefit. Check it out with your tax preparer before you assume that the mortgage company's estimate is accurate.

Determining a Price Range

The lending institution bases its answer to the "How much can you afford?" question on guidelines they have established statistically for themselves over the years. When a lender qualifies a borrower, they are telling that borrower the "maximum" amount they will lend to them, based upon their credit, income, and asset position. And frankly, not all households fit into the same mold. So before you can rely on a lender to tell you how much you can afford, you need to be able to answer the question for yourself. After all, the lender isn't the one responsible for paying your monthly obligations, you are.

And their "maximum" may be totally different than what you are comfortable with. For example, just because you and your partner can currently afford a $200,000 home doesn't mean that you should buy a $200,000 home. Maybe you're going to start a family, perhaps one of you wishes to change careers, or maybe one of your parents will need full-time nursing care. You cannot predict the future, but you can try to keep yourself within a "comfort zone" for monthly mortgage payments so you aren't living *house poor*.

Mortgage Speak

House poor refers to people who have bought more house than they really should have. Once people purchase a home and start filling it up with furniture and conveniences, it can sometimes preclude them from affording other things in their life. For example, they no longer have the disposable income for vacations, dinners out, or shopping. They start incurring credit card debt while trying to maintain a large mortgage payment.

Comparing Monthly Expenses

First-time home buyers tend to correlate their potential new mortgage payment with their present rent. On the surface this appears to be logical: substituting one housing expense for another. However, there is more to it than just that monthly expense.

Your mortgage payment to the lender is different from your rent or lease payment. In addition to the monthly payment of interest for the money you have borrowed, you will owe money that repays the

loan, known as the *principal*. The combination of
the two is commonly referred to as P&I. Also your
payment most likely will include monthly installments of taxes and property insurance, known in
the industry as T&I.

Mortgage Speak _____

Principal is the amount originally borrowed for the loan, excluding the interest.

The lender requires that you maintain homeowner's
insurance, also known as hazard insurance, on the
home at all times. In the event of a disaster, such as
a fire, there must be coverage to repair or replace
the dwelling at minimum. The coverage of your
belongings is optional, but of course you will want
those protected as well. Property taxes are also part
of a house payment to the lender, and these may
include school tax or city assessments particular to
your municipality.

Because a delinquent tax obligation may jeopardize
the lender's hold on the real estate, they always want
to make certain payments are maintained and
timely. Depending upon the type of loan, you may
also be responsible for a mortgage insurance premium monthly, known as *PMI* or *MIP*. This insurance is provided by a third party chosen by the
lender to reduce their risk in the loan.

There could be additional expenses associated with particular properties you may choose to purchase. Flood insurance would be required monthly if the home is in a designated flood plane. And there may be fees associated with a condominium complex or a neighborhood association to maintain common areas or amenities, such as foot paths or tennis courts.

Mortgage Speak

Private Mortgage Insurance (PMI) is risk insurance paid by the borrower to protect the lender if the loan should end in default and later go into foreclosure; insurance is required on loans with less than a 20 percent down payment. **FHA Mortgage Insurance Premium (MIP)** is insurance paid by the borrower on behalf of the lender to assure them if the loan defaults, the federal government insures the lender's indebtedness; 2.25 percent is added to the loan amount, .5 percent divided by 12 paid monthly.

We've compared the components of a payment, now let's look at the additional expenses. There is the new responsibility of maintenance and upkeep— both monetarily and perhaps physically. The days of phoning the landlord to fix the broken kitchen faucet or replace a torn screen door are gone! It will now be your responsibility to repair what is broken, or arrange for an upgrade to existing fixtures such as new countertops or flooring. That's not to say you cannot hire out the services should you not be qualified or able to perform the repair tasks; however, that is an experience and an expense that has not been realized up to this time for most renters.

And don't forget the fact that typically your home is larger than an apartment and therefore utility expenses will be higher than in the past, if you had to pay them at all! Even if you're purchasing an energy-efficient home, you cannot rely on the utilities to be less expensive for you. And there are those sewer charges, trash collection, and recycling services that become the homeowner's expense.

The Desire to Acquire

There are going to be things you will need, and things you will want. It's vital that you recognize the difference and prepare adequately for future expenses associated with any new acquisition. It's not often that a tenant has a rake for the lawn or a garden hose to rinse off the patio when living in a rental unit. Trash is usually placed into a dumpster, so there is no need for a trash receptacle. Exterior painting and lighting are maintenance issues for the landlord, not to mention the "fun" purchases that one can envision—wallpaper for the kitchen, new carpeting, and the perfect sofa to fit in the great room.

It's natural to look at a new home as just that: new! And new often means that you may want to purchase furnishings that may not have fit in your home previously or may not have been important up to now.

This "desire to acquire" tends to happen when you move into a home. So it's ever so important that thought be put into the timing of the purchases.

The Least You Need to Know

- You need to know what you can afford to pay; don't rely on the lender.
- Different parts of the country do things differently; you must learn the protocol for the housing market you are interested in purchasing in.
- Decipher what you need for your new home and what you may want; budget for your purchases and give careful consideration to how you are paying for them.

Chapter 2

Choosing a Lender

In This Chapter

- Different types of lenders
- Understanding the secondary market
- Finding the lender that fits

It can be intimidating to explore your finances on your own, let alone with a lender. You may wonder if your credit is acceptable, if you make enough money, or if you're too old to have a 30-year loan. You may be embarrassed by past credit history, or even worry about prejudices. And as you talk with family and friends about buying a home, everyone has his or her own stories to share, and some can be quite hair raising. It's no wonder that often people get to this point in the process and freeze.

Yet in most of the success stories, you'll find that the lender was the buyer's advocate in the process. Their job is to educate you, so that you're able to decide on the best loan product for your circumstances. The lender you choose should be knowledgeable about different loan programs and solutions, offering comparisons of why one may be more appropriate than another. He or she should never be condescending or judgmental. Most important, the lender should speak in a way that you understand. And if you are not familiar with a term or product, he or she should be approachable enough to ask to repeat what was said in "real words." This is why you should interview several people, because you'll find one who feels right, not just sounds good.

Types of Lenders

You have several different types of lenders to choose from. The mortgage market today looks very different than it did even 10 years ago, and it has evolved over a long period of time. It is helpful to understand where all these companies came from and how they are related to each other.

Banks

Banks have been the place to deposit and save money since the early 1800s and, in return, they pay us interest for using our money. Banks also lend money, taking their depositors' money and granting loans to others in return, being paid—with interest. So you could go to a bank, deposit your savings into a certificate of deposit earning 4 percent annually, and in turn, borrow money from the same bank and pay them 6 percent annually for the use of these funds.

Today, banks that lend in this fashion are known as *Portfolio Lenders*. They are creating their own lending practices according to their own risk management needs. Oftentimes, these borrowing requirements will appear to step outside of the norm, but still, the bank is assessing the risk and the likelihood of repayment. The approach is perhaps more individualized, and often a higher rate of interest may be assessed. It is like anything else; if custom made, it is probably more expensive.

Banks are also encouraged to create loan programs and lending practices that cater to their local neighborhoods. Known as the *Community Reinvestment Act* (*CRA*), banks are required to make certain that they are encouraging development of affordable single and multifamily (two to four units) housing. These loans target lending for low- to moderate-income households, and are intended to create more home ownership within the community. CRA loans may be offered at a lower interest rate, low to no down payment, and possibly with reduced fees to obtain the financing.

Mortgage Speak

A **Portfolio Lender** is a lender that makes loans, collects the payments, and uses their own funds rather than those available through the secondary market. The **Community Reinvestment Act** (**CRA**) is Federal legislation passed in 1977 to encourage open lending practices within an institution's immediate neighborhood or community.

Credit Unions

Credit unions became common loan resources in the 1930s. They were formed to provide services for people with a common background or affiliation, such as an association, a church, or an employer. The idea was to create credit cooperatives whereby you and other members could borrow money for prudent, worthwhile purposes and your character was more important than your ability to repay. Because you were borrowing your own as well as your fellow depositors' money, you were more likely to pay it back. An important difference between a bank and a credit union is that while the bank is looking for profit, the credit union is nonprofit. It is merely a service for its members.

It's Your Money

There are laws in place to protect you as the consumer, namely the Equal Credit Opportunity Act, enacted in 1974. This legislation was passed to assure a prospective borrower that he or she would be treated fairly without regard to race, age, gender, nationality, or marital status. The law prohibits a lender from making an arbitrary decision based upon one's dress or skin tone.

Credit unions offer a wide variety of loan products, including mortgages. When setting their lending practices, they typically lend based upon a combination of their own requirements and the guidelines and standards already set within their charter. Whereas banks that lend their portfolio follow their own rules, credit unions are perhaps a little more conservative because they have their depositors, or shareholders, to answer to. Some of the larger credit unions are beginning to access the secondary market as a source of mortgage lending capital. As with banks, credit unions are regulated by a branch of the federal government, the National Credit Union Administration.

Savings and Loans

The Savings and Loans (S&Ls) of the 1960s had the lending market cornered, along with commercial banks. Today they share the limelight with banks and mortgage companies but are still viable choices, and are typically located within your community.

The Savings and Loan Associations originated in the 1930s as a byproduct of the Great Depression. When the stock market crashed in 1929, banks were unable to provide depositors cash during the "run on the bank," and, therefore, faith in banking was lost. There was no money to spend and, therefore, no money to encourage growth and development.

The government stepped in to create the *FSLIC* (*Federal Savings & Loan Insurance Corporation*) and *FDIC* (*Federal Deposit Insurance Corporation*), which are the federal government's guarantees to banks and Savings and Loan depositors that funds placed into a savings institution would be safe and available to the depositor. The depositor feels better about leaving her money in the bank because she knows that it's guaranteed, and the banks don't need to worry about all their depositors making a run on the bank, draining their assets.

As people deposited money, these institutions were encouraged to turn around and lend for residential development. S&Ls became the primary resource for potential homeowners. As monies came in, monies were lent within the region, and market stability was re-established. Savings and Loans are highly regulated, and the government watches their lending habits closely to ensure depositors' protection.

Mortgage Speak

The **Federal Deposit Insurance Corporation (FDIC)** is a federal department for banking that insures up to $100,000 for depositors against loss. The **Federal Savings and Loan Insurance Corporation (FSLIC)** is a federal organization that insures deposits in savings and loans up to $100,000.

The savings and loan industry was deregulated in the 1970s so that it could compete with banking institutions. This new freedom led many toward new speculative real estate investments during an unstable economic period in the early 1980s. Loans were made in concentrated regions such as Texas, at a time when oil prices plummeted and foreclosures soared. And owners began using the S&Ls to fund their own real estate ventures, which were often very risky. The once closely watched S&L industry, although still regulated, ran amuck; many institutions became insolvent, causing the government to exercise the FSLIC guaranteed payout of $100,000 to depositors and realign the failed institutions with those still financially strong.

Mortgage Companies

Mortgage companies are in the business of making home loans, and they provide no other banking services. They lend monies from banks, pension funds, or insurance companies, and resell the mortgage paper to a third-party investor. Because they are not lending their own funds, mortgage companies are required to honor the guidelines set forth by their money source, known as the *secondary market* explained later in this chapter.

Mortgage Speak

The **secondary market** is the outlet for lenders to sell loans and recover their capital to lend again.

Other Lending Options

There are some other lending options available to you, for example, mortgage brokers, private investors, and investment firms.

Mortgage brokers are liaisons between the borrower and the money source. Typically they can offer loan products from several mortgage companies and banks, rather than from only one. The broker becomes familiar with the lending practices and the nuances of each institution, and determines which loan products may best suit your unique circumstances.

Private investors are also still available to some. They are individuals who make their own savings available to lend, with interest, of course. Because they lend their own money, they can make up their own qualification criteria, and charge an appropriate interest return based upon their perceived risk factor.

Investment firms have recently also entered the lending arena. A slightly different philosophy applies. Let's say that your savings are held in mutual funds and you don't want to liquidate. Some companies will lend to you based upon your portfolio holdings, securing your assets in return.

The Secondary Market

The secondary market developed in the 1960s as a government response to limited availability of mortgage lending capital. At the time, savings and loan institutions were the primary lenders to potential home buyers. And when a bank or savings and loan lend their money, they are taking on the entire burden of that note. In other words, if the loan is not paid the lender is left holding the bag. They were effective until inflation and growth within certain regional markets strained their resources, and many S&Ls were unable to meet the demands.

To increase the pool of available mortgage capital, the government intervened, creating the Federal National Mortgage Association. FNMA was later expanded into two divisions, *FNMA* and *GNMA* (Government National Mortgage Association). These institutions were given the authority to issue mortgage-backed securities. An investor could now choose to "invest" in mortgages, which was very attractive because mortgages had a predictable return (their rate of interest) and the mortgage-backed securities were a commodity with an implicit guaranty by the federal government. This generated more capital because investors trusted the return on investment, and, in turn, there was more money to lend to future borrowers, thus energizing the housing market.

Like FNMA and GNMA, the Federal Home Loan Mortgage Corporation (FHLMC) is a federally chartered agency. FHLMC was chartered by the federal government in 1970 as an additional resource for conventional financing at a time when demand was gaining for savings and loans and thrifts. As with FNMA and GNMA, FHLMC is highly regulated. FNMA and FHLMC are publicly traded and must operate and perform to a bottom line, because they are responsible to their shareholders. FNMA and FHLMC issue mortgage-backed securities collateralized by conventional loans. GNMA issues mortgage-backed securities collateralized by FHA and VA loans.

FNMA and FHLMC are often spoken of in the same breath because their guidelines and lending criteria are very similar. Although they cooperate on a limited basis with one another as they develop and grow, the two organizations are competitors for the same loans being originated by lenders. This competition benefits the consumer by driving down mortgage interest rates.

A final component of the secondary market is comprised of private issuers of mortgage-backed securities. These entities are primarily well-known Wall Street firms who purchase conventional, government, and so-called "private label" mortgage programs to be pooled for securitization.

Mortgage Speak

The **Federal National Mortgage Association (FNMA)**, known as Fannie Mae, is a federally chartered corporation created by Congress that provides conventional mortgage lending capital to mortgage bankers nationally. The **Federal Home Loan Mortgage Corporation (FHLMC)**, known as Freddie Mac, is also a federally chartered corporation that provides mortgage financing through the secondary market for conventional loans. The **Government National Mortgage Association (GNMA)**, known as Ginnie Mae, is a federal agency that supports the securitization of mortgage-backed securities collateralized by FHA and VA mortgage loans.

FNMA, FHLMC, and GNMA have standardized their lending criteria to assure their investors that the borrower will be able to repay his mortgage obligation, thus ensuring a predictable return on the investors' money. Those mortgage lenders who utilize the secondary market resources must abide by their lending rules or guidelines for that reason.

Comparing Lenders

With interest rates the last few years at unprecedented lows, everyone is in the business of lending these days. There are literally thousands of lenders to choose from, and surfing the net or letting your fingers do the walking in this instance is not the way to shop. Remember, this is the single most expensive purchase most folks make, so leave nothing to chance. Talk with others who have recently been through the home-buying process. Their experience is fresh, and if they've been advised properly, they've done their homework, too. Also, talk with your financial adviser, accountant, or attorney; they are great resources and often can offer names of local companies they've worked with in the past.

Be specific when asking for a referral. It's okay to know that the ABC Company provided great rates and service, but find out who at ABC Company they worked with. Usually a company will have several representatives, so if you're trying to replicate an experience, it's best to find the actual loan representative. If you just call into ABC Company, your experience may now be in the hands of the receptionist.

When interviewing the lender, ask the question, "How are you different?" and "What can you provide for me that another company cannot?" You may find, for example, because of your banking relationship, the mortgage company by the same name may provide you with a discount or lower fees. There may be a loan product specific to a lender that may be a perfect fit for your financing needs.

The Least You Need to Know

- There are different types of lending institutions, each with their own specific expertise.
- The secondary market resources such as FNMA, FHLMC, and GNMA provide money that will in turn be lent to you, so these resources create the guidelines for the primary lenders to follow.
- Interview a few different lenders, taking notes to use later to compare services, products, and so on.

Chapter **3**

Getting Pre-Approved

In This Chapter

- How the pre-approval process works
- Pre-approval benefits
- Pre-qualification vs. pre-approval
- Understanding the underwriting process

You've done your homework. You've taken charge of your price range by examining your personal finances. You've found a lender whom you trust and feel is working on your behalf to provide you the best possible loan package based upon your personal circumstances.

There are two parts to consider in the mortgage approval process. The first concerns you as the borrower: Are you likely to be able to repay the loan based upon your credit history, income, and debts today? The second part concerns the property you are purchasing: Is this real estate worth what the lender is lending to you (in case you cannot pay the payments, and the lender ends up with the house back) and is it a good property to secure the mortgage?

The answer to the first question can be found by getting pre-approved to purchase a home, which is the subject of this chapter. The second part of the approval takes place after you are approved, when you find the home you wish to purchase. The lender will evaluate the property and make certain it is a good risk for them to lend on. This process is known as the appraisal.

Pre-Qualification vs. Pre-Approval

The terms pre-qualification and pre-approval are often used interchangeably, but have two distinctively different meanings. A pre-qualification says that someone has discussed your finances with you, for example, income, assets, and debt. Based upon his opinion, you qualify to purchase a home in a certain price range. A pre-qualification validates that you are on the right path, but no actual review of documentation has taken place.

A pre-approval is a verification process. A lender has reviewed your pay stubs, W-2s, bank statements, and credit report, and he has approved you to borrow up to a certain amount, subject to a satisfactory review of the property to be purchased. There is usually a time limitation on this approval, based upon the age of the documentation provided. The lender may need to take another look at paystubs and bank account statements if more than 60 days elapse from the original approval, just to make certain there have been no significant changes in your financial picture.

Bet You Didn't Know

The concept of pre-approval is relatively new. Only in the last 10 years has the borrower had the option to apply for a loan either before or after they have entered into a contract to purchase a home. The pre-approval process is preferred by all parties: buyers, sellers, and real estate professionals. The pre-approval puts the financing up front, alleviating many of the questions later.

A pre-approval application mimics a real loan application, except that you are not in a firm contract to purchase a specific property yet. Following are the reasons why you want to be pre-approved before you are actively out shopping for a home:

- So that you're prepared. You know your price range, approximate monthly payment, out-of-pocket expenses, current market rates … you're armed with the information you need to make a legitimate, knowledgeable offer to a seller.

- To be in a better position to negotiate. The lender will provide you a letter of approval that verifies that you can qualify for the mortgage loan. The seller now knows something about you, if only that you are credit worthy to purchase his home. It's easier for the seller to negotiate with you, knowing that you are serious *and* have your money resources lined up.

- Save yourself heartache. Know the homes you look at are affordable and attainable to you before you fall in love and mentally move into them.

Now it's time to put your preliminary financing in place.

The Documentation

You're ready to put your paperwork on the table. So don't throw it out! Start a filing system, so that you're able to produce the proper supporting documentation to the lender. Here is information you are going to need:

- A full month of paystubs and two years of W-2s to verify your income

  If self-employed or paid by commission, provide complete tax returns for two years with all schedules and year-to-date profit/loss statement

- Two months of bank or investment account statements for your *assets*

- A list of all of your recurring monthly *liabilities*, their payments, and any approximate outstanding balances

- Additional verification that lenders may
  require based on your individual circumstances. Here are a few examples, but others
  are listed throughout this chapter:

  - Divorce Decree, Separation Agreement,
    or Child Support Order

  - Bankruptcy Schedule of Debtors and
    recorded Discharge

  - VA Discharge of Service (DD214) and
    Certificate of Eligibility

Mortgage Speak

Assets are everything that is owned and
tangible with a cash value. **Liabilities** are
debts that need to be repaid.

Income

Money that comes into your household may be
considered as income. Your income may be derived
from a job, pension, retirement, or social security.
Other sources could also be child support, alimony,
or ongoing proceeds received from an annuity or
trust fund. Rental income from investment real
estate, or royalties from something you have pro-
duced, such as published music or a book, can also
be considered if determined it is likely to continue.
The lender's objective is to determine that acceptable income will continue at its current level for a
period of time. Acceptable income is income derived
from a verifiable source.

In those instances where income has not been consistent (such as temporary employment assignments) or cannot be verified because the income is not claimed (as is the case with many restaurant servers), there are alternative means of verification of income discussed in Chapter 4.

Because most of us receive income from an employer, we will start with those requirements. The lender will ask to see your most recent pay stubs, in addition to W-2s from the previous year or two. It's important to note that she is looking at gross earnings, not net proceeds after taxes are deducted. If you've changed jobs in that window, provide her information from all employers. It's not frowned upon that job changes occur, but it's the lender's job to determine if the change was for the better. He is also looking for job growth. Irregular or inconsistent jobs send up a red flag.

Before You Sign

If your personal situation does not meet the lender's qualification criteria today, you may need to: (a) wait to apply for a home loan until you can establish the pattern necessary for the lender, usually 6 to 12 months; (b) consider an alternative loan program/product. Other financing solutions may exist, but because you're stepping outside the norm, you may pay slightly higher fees or see an increase in the interest rate.

If you were a student in that two-year window, you may be asked to provide transcripts. Education is often considered as part of your "job experience."

If you cannot locate your pay stubs and W-2s, be prepared to request duplicates, either from your employer or the Internal Revenue Service. In some cases, a letter from an employer spelling out the terms of your employment may be good enough, but it's likely you'll be asked to produce some sort of proof.

The lender may ask about any discrepancies between year-to-date income and monthly income. If income is low this year, has there been a recent increase in wages, or perhaps time off? If year-to-date income appears high based upon monthly earnings, has there been a bonus paid, or perhaps a cash-in of stock options? Also, if a raise is due within the next two to three months, try to provide a letter from your employer stating the terms of the increase. Those income dollars may be used in the qualification process if necessary.

If you receive social security or pension funds, the lender may ask to see a copy of the awards statement showing current amounts received, or, if directly deposited into your bank account, a copy of your bank statement. Trust income, child support, or alimony may require the lender have a copy of the decree that established the payment. Lender guidelines state that you must be able to show that proceeds are being received and that they are likely to continue for at least 12 months, the logic being that if you cannot show it, how can you count on it to help you repay your loan obligation.

> ### It's Your Money ___
>
> If you are expecting a bonus and would like to use it as a down payment, the lender can approve the mortgage subject to evidence of receipt. Be prepared to provide some proof from your employer that the funds are on their way. Some guidelines prohibit the lender from using a bonus as both income and an asset, so notify him up front so that he can decide whether you need the bonus income to qualify for the amount applied for.

Self-Employed Income

The documentation the lender needs is different if you are self-employed, because you cannot provide information from an outside source. You *are* your employer, so the burden of income verification lies with you. So for a conforming loan, he or she will be asking you for the same thing the government is asking for each year: your tax return (Form 1040 and all schedules). There are exceptions, but typically the lender wants to see a two-year history of self-employment. And if you're buying past mid-year, then be prepared to provide a year-to-date profit-and-loss statement showing how things are going since your last 1040 filing. A profit-and-loss lists earned income and expenses so far in the year. The lender will want to see that your income is more than your expenses. And rather than the gross sales amount, he or she is using the net effective income, after expenses, that the business incurred to earn the income.

Proceeds from the Sale of Your Current Home

When you sell real estate you own, the income received from that sale can then be used towards a new home purchase. The *proceeds*, as they are known, are recognized as profit or may be recovered capital from the original purchase of the property. It's not uncommon for a new home purchase to be dependent, or *contingent* on the sale of an existing home; the proceeds are needed for the down payment and costs associated with the purchase on the new home.

When a purchase contract is submitted from buyer to seller, there are usually stipulations that must be met or the contract may be dissolved. Commonly know in the real estate industry, these *contingencies* may be:

- The ability to obtain satisfactory financing.
- The completion of satisfactory inspections, such as termite, radon, or a complete home review.
- The contract may also be written contingent upon review of the document by legal counsel.
- The ability to close the transaction within a specified time noted in the contract.
- The satisfactory sale and close of a present residence because those proceeds are needed to perform the purchase of the new home.

If money is needed, and the home is not sold, usually someone involved in the transaction mentions a *bridge loan*. Bridge loan financing means that you are going to take the equity from one property and use it for the purchase of another property. At one time, the only way to extract income from a home was through a separate loan that only a select few lenders provided. The loan was meant to be a temporary loan, just until the property sold.

Since they offer a niche product, lenders charge higher fees to obtain these types of loans. Today, with the popularity of second mortgage financing, we have access as never before to the savings in our homes. A second mortgage is less expensive to obtain, requires little to no up front costs, and will provide the same access to equity as the bridge loan, for considerably less cost. So the popular bridge loan of years past has only remained in name.

Mortgage Speak

Bridge loan/bridge financing is a short term note to take equity from a present home for a down payment and fees for closing on a new home, rather than waiting for proceeds from the sale.

It's important to note here that whenever the bridge loan financing concept is offered, there are several important considerations. Let's say you have a home valued at $150,000, and expect to receive $40,000 in proceeds once it sells. Your expectation has been to use these monies for the purchase of your new home, but it hasn't sold yet. Bridge financing is a possibility.

Here is what happens: You have your present home and its payment. You are then going to obtain another loan on the home, a second mortgage to tap the $40,000. The balance on both loans will be paid off when this home sells, but in the mean time you have two mortgage payments. Now, as you qualify for the home, these monthly obligations are considered as ongoing and included in the overall debt ratios for approval, along with any auto loans, student loans, revolving credit debt, etc.

The good news is if you can qualify, you can purchase the new home regardless of whether your present residence sells. Then comes the question of comfort levels; do you feel equipped to make payments on both properties, should your first home not sell quickly? Is your disposable income in a place that can cover the extra expense for a time, or do you have savings available to help out while making the extra payment? This goes back to Chapter 2 and your budget. No matter what the lender says, it's you that makes the payments.

The other option is rather than sell your home, you may elect to keep it and rent it to others, hopefully to offset any expense or payment that is still out-standing. But if you need the equity from this home, and it is not going to be sold prior to closing on the new home, you may need to consider a more perma-nent financing solution, such as a refinance or a home equity loan to make funds available. In Chapter 10, there is a section that discusses comparing refinancing and home equity loans (seconds).

Assets

Assets are things you have that have a cash value. Examples of cash equivalent assets are checking, savings, CDs, stocks, savings bonds, and cash value of an insurance policy.

The lender will ask to see evidence of your money, so he or she will ask you to provide one to two months of your most recent bank/asset statements on any accounts that potentially could be used for the purpose of the purchase. If the bank statements have multiple pages, all pages must be received. Any irregular or recent large deposits will need to be explained. The lender will ask for evidence of where money has moved from when it's apparent that the deposit was not typical, i.e., a payroll deposit. You may also need to provide information regarding any derogatory data, such as an insufficient-funds notification.

If you cannot locate this information, ask the bank or financial institution to duplicate the documents for you, and ask them to sign the document for authentication. Some Internet banking sites can also provide statements. Please note that your name, the financial institution's name, and the account number must all be present for the document to be valid.

Also considered as assets are your tangible property, such as real estate, automobiles, and jewelry, even a baseball card collection. It is possible to sell an asset or to borrow against an asset to secure cash needed for a home purchase. If you do wish to sell something, make certain you've kept a good record of the transfer. The lender will also ask you to prove the asset's value, so get a reliable appraisal before selling. For example, if you sell an extra automobile while considering a home purchase, keep a copy of the bill of sale and a copy of title to show the amount you received and the transfer of ownership. A copy of the Blue Book Value or a retail auto dealer's value assessment is also a good idea to have. Paper trails can be a handy way of explaining sudden debt reduction or increases in your bank balances.

The same paper trail is important should you have an asset that you can borrow against, such as another piece of real estate. The lender is particularly interested in your savings and wants to understand where any and all unusual deposits come from. If it is not apparent from the bank statements where the money is coming from for the purchase, you may be asked for additional information to verify the source of the funds. If there is cash that isn't attached to a payroll deposit, for example, the lender will ask you to show where it came from.

Individual Retirement Accounts (IRAs) and Roth retirement plans are not considered *liquid assets*, although their balance can influence a loan decision. But if you have additional assets, let the lender know. As lenders lean today toward "risk-based pricing," savings can compensate for other less positive conditions, making the qualification process easier. If you wish to withdraw your funds from these plans, the lender will adjust the available total vested amount by the 10 percent federal withdrawal penalty and any applicable taxes. Due to the stiff penalties, IRAs are not thought to be the best source of capital with which to purchase a home.

There are, however, employer 401(k) plans that allow you to borrow against the vested amount. By borrowing against your secured asset (the 401[k]), you are using your own money and paying yourself back for the loan. It's important to visit with your plan administrator and learn about the possibilities and about your plan's loan restrictions, because they can vary significantly. Some may allow only quarterly withdrawals, whereas others may specify that you provide them with detailed information on the mortgage before allowing the withdrawal. In other words, you will need to have chosen the house and negotiated the terms of the purchase, and need to have chosen your lender and negotiated the loan program, before applying for the loan. You may also be prohibited from participating in your 401(k) program for a specified time. So weigh the pros and cons of this process before committing to a home. You'll need to know where your money is coming from for the purchase, and it is smart to only rely on the 401(k) if you've done your homework on the plan.

Mortgage Speak

Liquid assets are assets readily available to you, such as money in checking, savings, mutual funds, and money market accounts. Funds not considered liquid are those that have restricted access, such as certificates of deposit, retirement accounts, savings bonds, and stocks.

Liabilities

A liability is considered an ongoing payment obligation that you have to someone for something they have provided to you. Liabilities include rent, utilities, credit card payments, and installment loans. Liabilities are also debts incurred for services rendered, such as insurance or doctor bills.

Debts that a lender considers for his qualification guidelines are those monthly obligations paid to outside vendors that are not housing related, for example, rent, utilities, insurance, etc., that are expected to be paid monthly. It's a good idea to have a list prepared of all creditors, their minimum monthly payments, and balances available at application. Remember to add everyone you have an obligation with, including child support. The lender will be verifying your debts by ordering a credit report. The credit-reporting agencies may not have all monthly obligations listed; for example, some credit unions do not report to the bureaus. Court-ordered payments, such as child support and alimony, also may not appear on the report.

The lender is looking to determine how much you are presently obligated to pay out monthly, and how much you can conceivably be expected to carry based upon your income. Statistical analysis and historical data have established the guides the lender will follow to determine if you are qualified for the amount of house payment you have applied to receive.

The lender will also review your credit file to see your payment history, and he'll itemize any outstanding debts reported. If there are matters that need to be addressed on the credit report, or concerns about your overall credit, you should be notified of them at this point. The pre-approval loan process is done to confirm your ability to finance a home, so you will be notified of anything in your credit history that could potentially keep you from making your purchase. The lender will openly discuss all items with you pertaining to the report, and offer suggestions to you. It's not unusual to find discrepancies on the report, and you may be asked to clarify, explain, or assist in the removal of something not correctly reported.

You may be asked to write a letter of explanation addressing issues that may appear, such as late payments, derogatory history, or new accounts.

It's Your Money

If you've received your credit report recently, let your lender know! She can sometimes answer general questions by viewing your report. She will need to eventually pull her own report, however, because the Credit Reporting Act/Right to Privacy states that only the party requesting the report has access to the information.

Other Verifications

You may be asked to provide evidence of satisfactory rental payments to a present or previous landlord. Compile the last 12 months of cancelled checks (or bank statements showing the monthly debit if you do not receive the checks), or the name and address of the landlord to verify rental payments. It's also a good idea anytime you're trying to establish your credit worthiness to ask for letters of recommendations, be it from your landlord or anyone else you may have paid monthly installments to for a service or product.

If funds are coming from another source other than savings, you will be asked to provide evidence of cash to close. Gifts are common sources of funds for purchases, but may be handled differently depending on the type of loan you are applying for. In some cases, the down payment may also be obtained from a non-profit resource. It's important that you openly discuss the source of funds with your lender because some loans require that the borrower also has funds of his or her own as part of the purchase.

It's Your Money

To remove a party from his or her ownership, perhaps due to a divorce or separation, a quitclaim deed may be filed. This document releases the party's interest, or claim to the property. Even though you give up your right to the home, if the mortgage loan were to go into default and not be paid as agreed, it is possible the lender may come back to try and recover damages if you still appear on the mortgage. The only way to eliminate your obligation totally is to refinance, removing yourself from the loan entirely.

If recently divorced, you may be asked to provide a copy of your divorce decree as evidence for any obligations associated with that separation, such as child support, alimony, or separate maintenance.

If recently bankrupt, you may be asked for copies of the bankruptcy schedules, along with a copy of the Discharge of Debtor. You may also be asked to provide a letter of explanation on the circumstances surrounding the bankruptcy. Lending after a severe credit disturbance may be handled differently, based upon the causes and ultimate resolution of the bankruptcy, and the time since the completion of the action. Read more on this in Chapter 5.

Completing the Loan Application

Once the lender receives the appropriate documentation, he or she completes a brief interview and completes a *uniform residential loan application*, also known as a 1003 (to Fannie Mae). This standard form is used by lenders coast to coast.

Section I. Type of Mortgage and Terms of Loan: Indicate the type of loan applied for and the term of the mortgage, the interest rate, and amount borrowed.

Section II. Property Information and Purpose of Loan: List the property address along with the age of the home. You are also going to choose how you wish to hold title, or take ownership of the property.

Uniform Residential Loan Application

This application is designed to be completed by the applicant(s) with the lender's assistance. Applicants should complete this form as "Borrower" or "Co-Borrower", as applicable. Co-Borrower information must also be provided (and the appropriate box checked) when ☐ the income or assets of a person other than the "Borrower" (including the Borrower's spouse) will be used as a basis for loan qualification or ☐ the income or assets of the Borrower's spouse will not be used as a basis for loan qualification, but his or her liabilities must be considered because the Borrower resides in a community property state, the security property is located in a community property state, or the Borrower is relying on other property located in a community property state as a basis for repayment of the loan.

I. TYPE OF MORTGAGE AND TERMS OF LOAN

Mortgage Applied for:	☐ V.A. ☐ FHA	☐ Conventional ☐ FmHA	☐ Other:	Agency Case Number	Lender Case Number
Amount $	Interest Rate %	No. of Months	Amortization Type:	☐ Fixed Rate ☐ GPM	☐ Other (explain): ☐ ARM (type):

Section I. Type of Mortgage and Terms of Loan.

II. PROPERTY INFORMATION AND PURPOSE OF LOAN

Subject Property Address (street, city, state, ZIP)				No. of Units

Legal Description of Subject Property (attach description if necessary)

Year Built

Purpose of Loan	☐ Purchase	☐ Construction	☐ Other (explain):	Property will be:
	☐ Refinance	☐ Construction-Permanent		☐ Primary Residence ☐ Secondary Residence ☐ Investment

Complete this line if construction or construction-permanent loan.

Year Lot Acquired	Original Cost	Amount Existing Liens	(a) Present Value of Lot	(b) Cost of Improvements	Total (a+b)
	$	$	$	$	$

Complete this line if this is a refinance loan.

Year Acquired	Original Cost	Amount Existing Liens	Purpose of Refinance	Describe Improvements ☐ made ☐ to be made
	$	$		Cost $

Title will be held in what Name(s)	Manner in which Title will be held	Estate will be held in:
		☐ Fee Simple ☐ Leasehold (show expiration date)

Source of Down Payment, Settlement Charges and/or Subordinate Financing (explain)

Section II. Property Information and Purpose of Loan.

Section III. Borrower Information: If the borrower is in contract to purchase a home, then the details are taken from the purchase contract; otherwise, fill this in accurately.

Section IV. Employment Information: List where you work and for how long, your job title, and how much you've earned monthly. You will be asked to provide two years' worth of history.

Section V. Monthly Income and Combined Housing Expense Information: The lender will use the income documents and W-2s provided for this calculation. Any supplemental earnings from sources other than employment are noted here as well. To the right of the income is a side-by-side comparison of housing expenses, today and proposed. You'll note that taxes, insurance, mortgage insurance, and association dues are included in the proposed expense.

Section VI. Assets and Liabilities: The credit report is the key document that the lender will use to reconcile the information that you provide to them. As far as listing your assets, cash as well as personal property value can be included here. The cash portion is verified through the banking and asset statements you provide. You will be asked to ballpark your personal property values as well as your automobiles. There is a calculation of net worth at the bottom, which is the difference between assets and liabilities. Hopefully this is a positive number. If you own any other real estate, this will also be the place to list the property address and value/mortgage/rental income.

III. BORROWER INFORMATION

Borrower	Co-Borrower
Borrower's Name (include Jr. or Sr. if applicable)	Co-Borrower's Name (include Jr. or Sr. if applicable)

Social Security Number	Home Phone (incl. area code)	Age	Yrs. School	Social Security Number	Home Phone (incl. area code)	Age	Yrs. School
☐ Married ☐ Unmarried (include single, divorced, widowed) ☐ Separated	Dependents (not listed by Co-Borrower) no. ___ ages ___			☐ Married ☐ Unmarried (include single, divorced, widowed) ☐ Separated	Dependents (not listed by Borrower) no. ___ ages ___		
Present Address (street, city, state, ZIP) ☐ Own ☐ Rent ___ No. Yrs.				Present Address (street, city, state, ZIP) ☐ Own ☐ Rent ___ No. Yrs.			

If residing at present address for less than two years, complete the following:

Former Address (street, city, state, ZIP) ☐ Own ☐ Rent ___ No. Yrs.	Former Address (street, city, state, ZIP) ☐ Own ☐ Rent ___ No. Yrs.
Former Address (street, city, state, ZIP) ☐ Own ☐ Rent ___ No. Yrs.	Former Address (street, city, state, ZIP) ☐ Own ☐ Rent ___ No. Yrs.

Section III. Borrower Information.

Borrower		IV. EMPLOYMENT INFORMATION	Co-Borrower		
Name and Address of Employer	☐ Self Employed	Yrs. on this job	Name and Address of Employer	☐ Self Employed	Yrs. on this job
		Yrs. employed in this line of work/profession			Yrs. employed in this line of work/profession
Position/Title/Type of Business	Business Phone (incl. area code)		Position/Title/Type of Business	Business Phone (incl. area code)	

If employed in current position for less than two years or if currently employed in more than one position, complete the following:

Name and Address of Employer	☐ Self Employed	Dates(from-to)	Name and Address of Employer	☐ Self Employed	Dates(from-to)
		Monthly Income $			Monthly Income $
Position/Title/Type of Business	Business Phone (incl. area code)		Position/Title/Type of Business	Business Phone (incl. area code)	
Name and Address of Employer	☐ Self Employed	Dates(from-to)	Name and Address of Employer	☐ Self Employed	Dates(from-to)
		Monthly Income $			Monthly Income $
Position/Title/Type of Business	Business Phone (incl. area code)		Position/Title/Type of Business	Business Phone (incl. area code)	

Freddie Mac Form 65   10/92

Page 1 of 4   Borrower _____

Co-Borrower _____

Fannie Mae Form 1003   10/92

Section IV. Employment Information.

V. MONTHLY INCOME AND COMBINED HOUSING EXPENSE INFORMATION						
Gross Monthly Income	Borrower	Co-Borrower	Total	Combined Monthly Housing Expense	Present	Proposed
Base Empl. Income*	$	$	$	Rent	$	$
Overtime				First Mortgage (P&I)		
Bonuses				Other Financing (P&I)		
Commissions				Hazard Insurance		
Dividends/Interest				Real Estate Taxes		
Net Rental Income				Mortgage Insurance		
Other (before completing, see the notice in "describe other income," below)				Homeowner Assn. Dues		
				Other		
Total	$	$	$	Total	$	$

*Self Employed Borrower(s) may be required to provide additional documentation such as tax returns and financial statements.

Describe Other Income   Notice: Alimony, child support, or separate maintenance income need not be revealed if the Borrower(B) or Co-Borrower(C) does not choose to have it considered for repaying this loan.

B/C		Monthly Amount
		$

Section V. Monthly Income and Combined Housing Expense Information.

Section VI. Assets and Liabilities (part 1).

VI. ASSETS AND LIABILITIES

This statement and any applicable supporting schedules may be completed jointly by both married and unmarried Co-borrowers if their assets and liabilities are sufficiently joined so that the Statement can be meaningfully and fairly presented on a combined basis; otherwise separate Statements and Schedules are required. If the Co-Borrower section was completed about a spouse, this Statement and supporting schedules must be completed about that spouse also.

Completed ☐ Jointly ☐ Not Jointly

ASSETS	Cash or Market Value	LIABILITIES	Monthly Payt. & Mos. Left to Pay	Unpaid Balance
Description		Liabilities and Pledged Assets. List the creditor's name, address and account number for all outstanding debts, including automobile loans, revolving charge accounts, real estate loans, alimony, child support, stock pledges, etc. Use continuation sheet, if necessary. Indicate by (*) those liabilities which will be satisfied upon sale of real estate owned or upon refinancing of the subject property.		
Cash deposit toward purchase held by:	$			
		Name and address of Company	$ Payt./Mos.	$
List checking and savings accounts below				
Name and address of Bank, S&L, or Credit Union				
		Acct. no.		
Acct. no.	$	Name and address of Company	$ Payt./Mos.	$
Name and address of Bank, S&L, or Credit Union				
		Acct. no.		
Acct. no.	$	Name and address of Company	$ Payt./Mos.	$
Name and address of Bank, S&L, or Credit Union				
		Acct. no.		
Acct. no.	$	Name and address of Company	$ Payt./Mos.	$
Name and address of Bank, S&L, or Credit Union				

		Acct. no.		
Acct. no.	$	Name and address of Company	$ Payt./Mos.	$
Stocks & Bonds (Company name/ number & description)	$			
		Acct. no.		
Life insurance net cash value	$	Name and address of Company	$ Payt./Mos.	$
Face amount: $				
Subtotal Liquid Assets	$			
Real estate owned (enter market value from schedule of real estate owned)	$	Acct. no.		
Vested interest in retirement fund	$	Name and address of Company	$ Payt./Mos.	$
Net worth of business(es) owned (attach financial statement)	$			
Automobiles owned (make and year)	$			
		Acct. no.		
		Alimony/Child Support/Separate Maintenance Payments Owed to:	$	
Other Assets (itemize)	$			
		Job Related Expense (child care, union dues, etc.)	$	
		Total Monthly Payments	$	
Total Assets a.	$	**Net Worth (a-b)** ▸ $	**Total Liabilities b.**	$

Freddie Mac Form 65   10/92   Page 2 of 4   Borrower _____   Co-Borrower _____   Fannie Mae Form 1003   10/92

Section VI. Assets and Liabilities (part 2).

VI. ASSETS AND LIABILITIES (cont.)

Schedule of Real Estate Owned (if additional properties are owned, use continuation sheet)

Property Address (enter S if sold, PS if pending sale or R if rental being held for income)	Type of Property	Present Market Value	Amount of Mortgages & Liens	Gross Rental Income	Mortgage Payments	Insurance, Maintenance, Taxes & Misc.	Net Rental Income
		$	$	$	$	$	$
Totals		$	$	$	$	$	$

List any additional names under which credit has previously been received and indicate appropriate creditor name(s) and account number(s):

Alternate Name	Creditor Name	Account Number

Section VI. Assets and Liabilities (part 3).

Section VII. Details of Transaction: A list of costs of the loan is a summary of the Good Faith Estimate. The sales price is added to the closing costs and prepaid expenses. The mortgage amount is subtracted, and the borrower's required cash to close is noted.

Section VIII. Declarations: You will be asked to answer several questions. The material you provide to the lender will answer a lot of what he needs to know about you to determine your credit worthiness. There are, however, items that are unknown that he will directly ask you about. If you answer yes to any of these, other than those regarding U.S. citizenship, previous homeownership, and whether you intend to live in the home, you will be asked to explain. And perhaps this may have a bearing on your qualification. By answering these questions, the lender finds out things he may not otherwise learn from the documents you have provided. Because lending guides are so specific, your lender may learn something that would cause him to redirect you into another loan solution.

Section IX. Acknowledgment and Agreement: Read the paragraph, and all parties sign if you agree to the terms.

VII. DETAILS OF TRANSACTION	$
a. Purchase price	
b. Alterations, improvements, repairs	
c. Land (if acquired separately)	
d. Refinance (incl. debts to be paid off)	
e. Estimated prepaid items	
f. Estimated closing costs	
g. PMI, MIP, Funding Fee	
h. Discount (if Borrower will pay)	
i. Total costs (add items a through h)	
j. Subordinate financing	
k. Borrower's closing costs paid by Seller	
l. Other Credits (explain)	
m. Loan amount (exclude PMI, MIP, Funding Fee financed)	
n. PMI, MIP, Funding Fee financed	
o. Loan amount (add m & n)	
p. Cash from/to Borrower (subtract j, k, l & o from i)	

VIII. DECLARATIONS	Borrower		Co-Borrower	
If you answer "yes" to any questions a through i, please use continuation sheet for explanation.	Yes	No	Yes	No
a. Are there any outstanding judgments against you?	☐	☐	☐	☐
b. Have you been declared bankrupt within the past 7 years?	☐	☐	☐	☐
c. Have you had property foreclosed upon or given title or deed in lieu thereof in the last 7 years?	☐	☐	☐	☐
d. Are you a party to a lawsuit?	☐	☐	☐	☐
e. Have you directly or indirectly been obligated on any loan which resulted in foreclosure, transfer of title in lieu of foreclosure, or judgment? (This would include such loans as home mortgage loans, SBA loans, home improvement loans, educational loans, manufactured (mobile) home loans, any mortgage, financial obligation, bond, or loan guarantee. If "Yes," provide details, including date, name and address of Lender, FHA or VA case number, if any, and reasons for the action.)	☐	☐	☐	☐
f. Are you presently delinquent or in default on any Federal debt or any other loan, mortgage, financial obligation, bond, or loan guarantee? If "Yes," give details as described in the preceding question.	☐	☐	☐	☐
g. Are you obligated to pay alimony, child support, or separate maintenance?	☐	☐	☐	☐
h. Is any part of the down payment borrowed?	☐	☐	☐	☐
i. Are you a co-maker or endorser on a note?	☐	☐	☐	☐
j. Are you a U. S. citizen?	☐	☐	☐	☐
k. Are you a permanent resident alien?	☐	☐	☐	☐
l. Do you intend to occupy the property as your primary residence? If "Yes," complete question m below.	☐	☐	☐	☐
m. Have you had an ownership interest in a property in the last three years?	☐	☐	☐	☐
(1) What type of property did you own—principal residence (PR), second home (SH), or investment property (IP)?	___		___	
(2) How did you hold title to the home-solely by yourself (S), jointly with your spouse (SP), or jointly with another person (O)?	___		___	

Section VII. Details of Transaction. Section VIII. Declarations.

IX. ACKNOWLEDGMENT AND AGREEMENT

The undersigned specifically acknowledge(s) and agree(s) that: (1) the loan requested by this application will be secured by a first mortgage or deed of trust on the property described herein; (2) the property will not be used for any illegal or prohibited purpose or use; (3) all statements made in this application are made for the purpose of obtaining the loan indicated herein; (4) occupation of the property will be as indicated above; (5) verification or reverification of any information contained in the application may be made at any time by the Lender, its agents, successors and assigns, either directly or through a credit reporting agency, from any source named in this application, and the original copy of this application will be retained by the Lender, even if the loan is not approved; (6) the Lender, its agents, successors and assigns will rely on the information contained in the application and I/we have a continuing obligation to amend and/or supplement the information provided in this application if any of the material facts which I/we have represented herein should change prior to closing; (7) in the event my/our payments on the loan indicated in this application become delinquent, the Lender, its agents, successors and assigns, may, in addition to all their other rights and remedies, report my/our name(s) and account information to a credit reporting agency; (8) ownership of the loan may be transferred to successor or assign of the Lender without notice to me; (9) the Lender, its agents, successors and assigns make no representations or warranties, express or implied, to the Borrower(s) regarding the property, the condition of the property, or the value of the property.

Certification: I/We certify that the information provided in this application is true and correct as of the date set forth opposite my/our signature(s) on this application and acknowledge my/our understanding that any intentional or negligent misrepresentation(s) of the information contained in this application may result in civil liability and/or criminal penalties including, but not limited to, fine or imprisonment or both under the provisions of Title 18, United States Code, Section 1001, et seq., and liability for monetary damages to the Lender, its agents, successors and assigns, insurers and any other person who may suffer any loss due to reliance upon any misrepresentation which I/we have made on this application.

Borrower's Signature	Date	Co-Borrower's Signature	Date
X		X	

Section IX. Acknowledgment and Agreement.

Section X. Information for Government Monitoring Purposes: This area of the application is set aside for borrower disclosure of race and sex. There are several race categories to choose from, and also an option to abstain. If you abstain from answering, the lender is still required to complete this portion to meet fair-lending criteria set forth by the federal government. Information about the interviewer, his or her phone number, and address are also noted in this section.

Continuation Sheet/Residential Loan Application: Your application may have additional pages that are carry-over sections. In other words, not all of your information fit into the sections available, so you have gone to an overflow section.

And of course, sign and date the bottom of the last page to indicate that the information you provided is accurate and true.

Bet You Didn't Know

> The practice of disclosure is not done to irritate the borrower, but rather to protect the borrower and future applicants. Loan applications are periodically audited by housing regulatory agencies to ensure that the lender is not "redlining," or selectively choosing to whom he or she will lend based upon race, gender, age, etc.

X. INFORMATION FOR GOVERNMENT MONITORING PURPOSES

The following information is requested by the Federal Government for certain types of loans related to a dwelling, in order to monitor the Lender's compliance with equal credit opportunity, fair housing and home mortgage disclosure laws. You are not required to furnish this information, but are encouraged to do so. The law provides that a Lender may neither discriminate on the basis of this information, nor on whether you choose to furnish it. However, if you choose not to furnish it, under Federal regulations this Lender is required to note race and sex on the basis of visual observation or surname. If you do not wish to furnish the above information, please check the box below. (Lender must review the above material to assure that the disclosure satisfy all requirements to which the Lender is subject under applicable state law for the particular type of loan applied for.)

BORROWER ☐ I do not wish to furnish this information

Race/National Origin:
☐ American Indian or Alaskan Native
☐ Black, not of Hispanic origin
☐ Asian or Pacific Islander
☐ White, not of Hispanic origin
☐ Hispanic
☐ Other (specify) _____

Sex: ☐ Female ☐ Male

CO-BORROWER ☐ I do not wish to furnish this information

Race/National Origin:
☐ American Indian or Alaskan Native
☐ Black, not of Hispanic origin
☐ Asian or Pacific Islander
☐ White, not of Hispanic origin
☐ Hispanic
☐ Other (specify) _____

Sex: ☐ Female ☐ Male

To be Completed by Interviewer	Interviewer's Name (print or type)	Name and Address Interviewer's Employer
This application was taken by: ☐ face-to-face interview ☐ by mail ☐ by telephone	Interviewer's Signature Date	
	Interviewer's Phone Number (incl. area code)	

Freddie Mac Form 65   10/92   Page 3 of 4   Fannie Mae Form 1003   10/92

Section X. Information for Government Monitoring Purposes.

Continuation Sheet/Residential Loan Application		
Use this continuation sheet if you need more space to complete the Residential Loan Application. Mark B for Borrower or C for Co-Borrower.	Borrower:	Agency Case Number:
	Co-Borrower:	Lender Case Number:

Continuation Sheet/Residential Loan Application.

Underwriting

The final review of the application and all of its supporting documentation is called *underwriting*. This analysis determines to what extent the lender may be risking his assets. The hope of every lender is that the monies lent to borrowers can be recovered through agreed-upon monthly payments over a predetermined period of time, or until such time that the note is satisfied. There are times that things don't always go as anticipated. It's the underwriter's job to assess the risk, to the best of her ability, based upon a snapshot in time.

Mortgage Speak

Underwriting is the analysis of information to determine a borrower's ability to repay an obligation based upon credit, employment, and assets, during a snapshot in time.

Underwriters are employees of the lender or individuals outside the company on contract, hired for the purpose of assessing risk on behalf of the lender.

Historically, underwriting has been done either by an individual or in a committee setting such as a board. In both cases, the decision was somewhat subjective, based upon the decision maker's previous experiences. And as with any human process, time was involved to receive, review, and render a decision, typically two to four days. Particularly with higher volumes due to the low-interest-rate climates today, time became a serious, negative aspect of underwriting.

As our technological advances have become more sophisticated, so has our ability to assess risk. Risk-based underwriting and credit scoring has become more prevalent in determining a borrower's qualification. In many cases, a lender today can render a decision on a file within hours of completing the application.

The documentation still needs to be looked at and validated by an underwriter, but his or her subjective opinion no longer makes the decision. The merit of the file is solely based upon its statistical composition, relative to other files that have like components, and that have been documented over a period of several decades. What this means to the borrower is a quicker loan decision on files that make sense.

But if, for whatever reason, a piece of their data doesn't fit within the box, such as a low credit score, all may not be rosy. The automated underwriting system, if it were the sole decision-making method, could possibly reject the loan. So it's still very important to have the opinion of the underwriter with the final say-so.

The pre-approval process only needs to be completed once for the borrower, assuming that the outcome is what the buyer anticipated. There are time limitations on the documents, so the borrower must purchase a home within a designated period of time. The lender should provide the borrower with a letter outlining the terms under which the approval is issued. It should include language about the lender needing to also inspect and approve any home to be purchased. Remember, you as the borrower are only half of the equation of the approval. The other half is the home.

Regulatory Disclosures and Disclaimers

The loan application is only the beginning of the process a lender must follow to complete your loan. The lending industry is highly regulated to protect the consumer against misrepresentation and fraud. Several regulatory disclosures and disclaimers will be presented throughout the process, but notice that this list may not include those items particular to your state's laws.

- Fair Lending—this document speaks to discriminatory lending practices.
- ECOA—this document refers to the Equal Credit Opportunity Act.
- Consumer Handbook for Adjustable Rate Mortgages (ARM loans only)—outlines the ins and outs of ARM loans.
- HUD Settlement Booklet (FHA loans only)— a complete guide to the process, provided by HUD.
- HMDA—you will receive this document if you are denied. It is a government credit denial notification.

What Standards Must Be Met for an Underwriter?

Traditionally, underwriting decisions were based upon a borrower's housing-expenses-to-income relationship, and his housing expense plus all his other monthly obligations in relationship to his income. The relationships, or ratios, listed here have been in place for a number of years. You will still hear them mentioned occasionally, but the industry is moving away from this method of qualification. Technology is advancing us; and, rather than using ratios, the industry is evaluating risks with computer-based automated underwriting systems which rely upon years of statistical loan performance. But for general purposes, you will find the information helpful in planning.

The following basic relationships are considered:

- Your housing expenses should not exceed 28 to 33 percent of your *gross monthly earnings*.

- Your housing expenses, in addition to all other *long-term debt*, should not exceed 36 to 41 percent of your gross monthly earnings.

Your housing expenses should not exceed 28 to 33 percent of your gross monthly earnings. This includes the following:

- **Principal and interest.** This calculation is the monthly amount the lender requires to repay the loan in the agreed amount of time.

- **Taxes.** One twelfth of annual property taxes
  are typically collected as part of the payment.
  Note that the lender requires evidence that
  all taxes are paid current on the property to
  prevent unnecessary tax liens on the home,
  thus guaranteeing their first lien position.

Mortgage Speak

Gross monthly earnings are defined as
stable, predictable earnings. Salary or
hourly income falls within this category,
and is usually taken at face value if there
is a history. If you're paid overtime, bonus,
and/or commissions, you can expect to
provide earnings information for two years,
which will then be averaged. **Long-term
debt** is defined as all revolving debt, and
any installment debt that has more than 10
months remaining. An example of revolving credit would be a credit card that has
a balance and interest rate that fluctuates
based upon usage and payments. Installment debt is repaid on a preset schedule,
each month, for a specific period of time.
Add in child support, alimony, and separate maintenance, if applicable.

It's Your Money

If you have 20 percent for a down payment, you may request to pay your own taxes and insurance rather than have the lender collect monthly (known as escrow). If you choose not to escrow you have your money and can earn interest on it as well as manage when the payments to the county and insurance company are made. On the down side, taxes and insurance are typically required in lump sum payments, so you may find it more comfortable to plan for them in the budget by allowing the lender to collect the amounts monthly.

- **Insurance.** One twelfth of annual homeowner's insurance premium is required to be part of the payment the lender receives. Note that the lender requires that at minimum fire insurance coverage be in place on the dwelling at all times. If the lender is ever notified of a lapse of insurance, there is a policy put into place immediately to cover the structure. Should there be any damage due to fire or weather-related elements, the lender wants coverage to repair or replace the dwelling if needed.

- **PMI/MIP.** This is a risk insurance known as Private Mortgage Insurance (PMI) on conventional loans and Mortgage Insurance Premium (MIP) on FHA loans.

These risk insurances are required by the lender to mitigate the risk on a loan to a borrower with less than a 20 percent down payment. This type of insurance is meant to offset the lender's exposure in the event the borrower defaults on the loan and the lender has no choice but to pursue a foreclosure. In the event of a foreclosure, a lender may only recover 70 to 75 percent of the original appraised value due to accrued interest, attorney fees, maintenance, and marketing costs. Lender's mortgage insurance offsets these expenses in the event of a claim. Lenders do not want you to walk away from your obligation of repayment because they would ultimately end up with the home and they are not in the business of owning real estate.

- **Flood Insurance.** It is possible that the home you choose to purchase may be located in a flood plane, and if so, you may be required to obtain flood insurance before the lender will finalize the loan. Your insurance provider can assist you in obtaining this government-guaranteed policy.

- **Homeowner's Association Dues.** These are fees associated with your housing development, typically paid for maintenance and up-keep for common amenities, such as a pool or a clubhouse. These fees are not collected by the lender but paid directly to the association. But because they are an added expense for the property, the fee is considered when calculating the housing expense.

Bet You Didn't Know

Contrary to popular belief, flooding is not covered typically as part of your homeowner's insurance policy. You may possibly have coverage if there is related wind or weather damage. Most insurance carriers provide policy riders to add for some flood damage, for example, if a sump pump should fail during a storm.

Your housing expenses (all the previously listed expenses) in addition to all other long-term debt (car payments, personal loans, etc.) should not exceed 36 to 41 percent of your gross monthly earnings. The 5 percent difference (41 to 36) depends upon the loan type and the down payment on each loan product. When in doubt, hit the middle.

In the table that follows, as an example, let's say you earn $4,500/month and you pay out monthly $569 in a car loan, student loan, and credit debt.

Gross Monthly Income		$4,500.00*__(A)
Housing Expense: Monthly		
	P&I	$871.75
	Taxes	$200.00
	H.O. Ins.	$40.00
	PMI/MIP	$65.00
	Total	$1,176.75__(B)

Recurring Debts: Monthly Pmts.

Auto	$320.00
Student Loan	$125.00
Credit Card	$45.00
Personal Loan	$79.00
Child Support	
Alimony	
Other	
Total	$569.00__(C)

Total (B) + (C) $1,745.75__(D)

(B) ÷ (A) 1176 ÷ 4500 = 26.13**

(D) ÷ (A) 1526 ÷ 4500 = 38.79***

Calculated based upon hourly earnings or an average of previous two year's earnings
**Should not exceed 28 to 33%*
***Should not exceed 36 to 40%*

Aside from the ratios, the underwriter will look for stability in employment, good credit, and any assets to close that are available and verifiable.

Keep in mind that this is not the way loans are approved or denied today, and are only meant as a guide. I stress this because if you do fall outside of the box here, it may be of no consequence. When your scenario is run through the computer's decision engine, it takes into account your circumstances, and it will decide whether you are a satisfactory credit risk.

And what if the computer and the underwriter, after careful consideration, do not approve your loan request? The lender is required to present you a detailed explanation of why he or she cannot grant you a loan. And if credit related, you can request a free copy of the report be issued to you.

The Least You Need to Know

- The pre-approval process is meant to take the guesswork out of purchasing a home; you will be fully aware of fees, payments, and how much home to look at before becoming emotionally attached to something out of your price range.

- Once there were set qualification guidelines; today automated approval systems that have compiled historic statistical data make many underwriting decisions. Therefore you cannot rely on the ratio method of qualification that has guided homebuyers for the last two decades.

- The lender will ask you to provide detailed information and documentation with regards to your income assets and debt, so take time to compile the proper paperwork, but be prepared for the barrage of questions.

Knowing Your Options—
If You Don't Fit the Mold

In This Chapter

- When you're not the perfect customer for a mortgage
- If you don't have all the right pieces of paper
- The impact of bankruptcy and credit counseling
- How to manage a poor credit report

What happens if your calculation for a house exceeds what the lender believes you're capable of paying monthly? Or you don't have all of the paperwork necessary to properly document the file? Does that mean you cannot get a mortgage loan? Absolutely not!

The pre-approval process from Chapter 3 was meant to prepare a potential homebuyer for a purchase, and that may mean there's still some work to do, or perhaps you might need an alternative loan solution. It's always better to know where you stand up front, before you have become emotionally involved with a potential home. This chapter offers suggestions on how to get financed if your circumstances don't meet the industry model.

Understanding Prime and Subprime Loans

The industry has changed dramatically in the last 20 years, and it's almost as if two lending practices have evolved out of one. Conforming loans are traditional, good-credit, verifiable-income loans. These loans meet most lenders' requirements and there's nothing unusual about the file. These borrowers can expect the best terms and lowest interest rates because of their desirability. These loans are also known as *A* paper loans, or prime loans.

It's Your Money

Credit is rated, with **A** being the best, **A–** being a few credit slips, and **B/C** credit showing several late payments, derogatory creditor comments, perhaps even collections and bankruptcy. As your credit slips from perfect, the interest rates rise, as much as several percentage points higher than for perfect credit.

Loans that don't meet traditional standards because of their derogatory credit (missed payments) or slow pays (late payments) are categorized as *B/C* loans. And these B/C loans have found a home in the sub-prime lending market. The subprime lending market refers again to the rating of the loan. Prime is a loan that fits standard lending practices and a sub-prime refers to loans that are outside the standard lending arena.

Subprime lending works for the borrower who may have slow pays on their credit reports, no verifiable cash, or perhaps has self-employed income for less than two years. And because they don't fit the model, lenders who choose to finance these borrowers will often collect a premium on rate. For example, a loan that fits the model may be offered for a stan-dard 6 percent interest rate, while a subprime loan might warrant an 8 percent interest rate. In other words, expect to pay more for the exception, just as you would if you were to order a tailor-made suit. When you require a custom product, you will pay extra for that service.

And just because you fall into the subprime category doesn't preclude you from shopping for the best possible financing package. Look at other rates and programs that may be available. Because there is a push towards anti-predatory lending legislation, awareness to unfair lending practices is at an all-time high. Anti-predatory in this sense means that the industry should be forbidden to take advantage of a captive and often desperate audience, or group of borrowers who might feel unable to overcome their circumstances by any other means than to pay exorbitant fees. But this has not kept all unscrupulous lenders out of the arena. Fortunately, there are several federal mandates that create opportunities to compare rates, as you will see in Chapter 5.

The cost of these B/C loans will vary depending upon how severe the deviation from the norm. If you're in this group, then you'll need to learn another way of thinking, the alternative to what has been considered mainstream. We'll discuss the guidelines in this chapter so that you'll have an understanding of what other options are out there.

Common Problems

Before considering the alternative solutions, we'll work through common issues that may arise. But realize that there's a reason they call this an approval "process," because there are ongoing variables, and just as many solutions. Lenders are in the business of lending, and they will continue to evolve to service their customers as long as the borrower's circumstances require them to do so. And they truly want to loan money to the right borrower with the right circumstances.

You Cannot Provide the Necessary Documentation

So what do you do if you don't have all of your income and asset information? In many cases, the lender can help you obtain copies of your paperwork, and it's not uncommon for the lender to go directly to the source, let's say your employer, and ask them to verify your tenure, position, and income. The lender will ask you to sign a consent form to authorize him or her to obtain information on you. Written requests are made all of the time on behalf of borrowers. It's only been recently that borrowers provided the information rather than lenders obtaining it on their own.

But what if you cannot provide the documentation that will substantiate your income or assets? There are many lenders today who offer alternative means of verifying income. They've been known to use bank statements that show regular deposits to substantiate take-home pay.

There are also loans that will skip the verification process entirely, for a slightly higher rate of interest (called "no doc" loans). Stated programs allow the borrower to list both his income and assets without any paper trail. The program is meant to bypass the paperwork. It is not intended for the borrower who is tempted to fabricate or manipulate his qualification for a loan, but to assist qualified borrowers around the paperwork.

You Need a Co-Mortgagor

If you don't make enough money on your own to qualify for the mortgage, there is the possibility a co-mortgagor would help your cause. The co-mortgagor should be a parent, relative, or someone you can substantiate a close relationship with, such as a partner. There could also be a child as a co-mortgagor for a parent. The co-mortgagor will be asked to provide the same information that you have been asked to provide. There will be credit reports pulled for each of you, and a qualification process will begin based upon both of your financial histories. A co-borrower's circumstances are hopefully positive (good credit and assets). If acceptable, the co-borrower will sign all of the paperwork with the borrower.

It's important to note that the new mortgage obligation will appear on both borrowers' credit reports going forward. Also, if the payment is split between each borrower, the interest deduction can be split, based upon how much each of you has paid on the loan. In other words, the co-borrower receives a possible tax break. That may be an incentive for the co-borrower to add the helping hand.

You Have Too Much Debt

Consider consolidating or paying off some of your balances. If your overall cash flow can improve and debt can be reduced, qualification may be easier. Put a plan into motion to pay minimum payments on all debts, but pay as much as you can on one. By paying off even one credit card, psychologically, you're getting ahead of the interest game. After that debt is eliminated, take the extra cash and concentrate on the next obligation on the list.

It's important in the beginning to choose a realistic liability, say, the card with the lowest balance. As you experience the success of eliminating debts, you can then choose to pay off other debts, for example, those with the highest interest rate. The key to this method is to focus on each debt individually, rather than paying a little extra on all of your accounts.

It's Your Money

Don't hesitate to look for gift money from parents and relatives. If available, gifts can help to lighten the debt load for qualification.

Understanding Your Credit

Until the 1950s, most money-lending was done within the community you lived in. Everyone knew each other, and most business was sealed with a handshake. But as the credit card industry grew, and lending services expanded across state lines, the need for accurate credit reporting was developed.

Your credit report is available to you, and I strongly recommend that you take the time to preview it for accuracy. The first time you see your own report, you may be astounded at how much of "you" is available to anyone who is authorized to look.

By reviewing your own report, you will learn the importance of timely payments. Your creditor provides their data to the bureau, usually monthly. And it notes if the account is current, if the payment was received as agreed or late, and if late, how late. It's good information for the lender. In theory, if

you pay as agreed on other contracts, you'll probably be timely on your mortgage. And each payment
is reviewed, not just a yearly overview. So it's vital
to be diligent in bill paying.

Collections are also reported to the bureau with
contact information to help resolve disputes. There
is also a section of the report set aside for public-
record information; evictions, legal disputes, a
divorce, and tax liens all become part of your credit
report.

Reading a Credit Report

Each of the three large reporting services has its own
format, but the information is basically the same.

The credit bureau offering the information is listed
at the top, with the borrower's name and information directly beneath it. If there is any discrepancy
on how the name is spelled, or perhaps an alias that
doesn't fit into the regular pattern, an Alert is shown
to let the report's recipient know there may be a
possible conflict in information provided. The report
will list the employer and contact information if
retrieved. Credit scores are noted for each borrower
and for each of the three repositories that have provided information.

The reports may differ at this point, but all will
list the trade lines or creditors that you have established, the date credit was extended, how much
was lent, and how much is required to repay the
obligation. The history of how the payments have
been received by the creditor is also shown.

The report will also show if there are any mentions of the borrower in public records. This is when a divorce or bankruptcy may appear on the report. Each time a creditor looks at your credit history, an Inquiry is created, with the date it was made, by which reporting bureau, and for which creditor. This allows you to know exactly who has been given a copy of your credit history.

Somewhere on the report there is a summary of the accounts, broken down between revolving, installment, mortgage, and so on, so that the lender may see where the open credit risk lies. There is a summary of the derogatory accounts, and a listing to use if you'd like to contact the reporting bureaus for any additional details. Many reports today also provide individual account contacts. For example, if you have a Visa, they will list the address and phone number on the report if you have a question about how your account was reported.

The report can also tell you the accounts that are open and those that have been closed. This can be particularly helpful for reconciling—we all have opened accounts for the fabulous discount to purchase. This is a great time to review what may still be open and what needs to be open.

Your report is updated regularly. Each time you're billed by your creditor and you pay, they note the timeliness of your payment in their computer. Their computer then talks with the bureau's computer, and your file reflects the new information. This sounds simple until you multiply by three bureaus, because all three need the information. And if your creditor doesn't report to all three bureaus, then not all of the history is available. That's why it's a common practice for the lender to request a credit report that reflects information from all three bureaus, known as a tri-merge file.

It's Your Money

Credit fraud and stealing identities happen all too frequently. And often we can prevent misuse of our information by being aware of how we allow our credit data to be used. Take time to consider how many available credit cards you have in your name, and consider closing those not used. Also, know who you give your information to, particularly phone solicitations and Internet purchases.

If you find something reported incorrectly, the lender typically will help you forward your dispute to the credit bureau. The bureau is obliged to remove or correct any erroneous information in a timely manner. This can take some time, however, which is why it is a good idea to check your reports very early in your home-buying process.

Bet You Didn't Know _____

There are three major credit reporting
services (also known as credit repositories)
that provide information on your credit
history: Experian (1-888-397-3742),
TransUnion (1-800-888-4213), and
Equifax (1-800-685-1111). Most mortgage
lenders require a tri-merged credit search
(a peek from all three) when qualifying a
borrower.

Correcting Your Report

There are, on occasion, credit histories that get
crossed. As you would expect, criss-crossed credit
appears in families with "Jrs" or "Srs" or folks with
regular names such as James Smith. When a lender
requests the credit pull, he or she reviews the report
to see if it matches up with information the borrower has provided. If it doesn't, then inquiries are
made. The lender may need help to correct erroneous entries.

Divorce tends to muddy a credit report, also. It's
not unusual for spousal credit to appear on each
other's report. But when the client is divorced, a
divorce decree is usually required to explain who is
responsible for the debt. The mortgage lender will
only use debts that are part of the borrower's obligation, as long as they've been paid as agreed.

Something not all divorce attorneys will tell you is how important it is that you close out all joint accounts. Even though the mortgage lender will abide by the divorce decree when looking at debts, a creditor may choose never to release you from your obligation unless the account has been closed out. I've seen more than one ugly credit report where the disgruntled ex-spouse has set out to sabotage the other's credit by refusing to pay or by filing bankruptcy. In such a case, you are left holding the bag, even if your remaining credit is spotless.

If you discover that incorrect information is on your credit report that may negatively influence your score, you may dispute and ask for a correction. Under the *Fair Credit Reporting Act*, the reporting bureau is permitted 30 days to investigate and correct erroneous information. Once the information has been corrected, then a new credit score can be obtained. Note that each of the credit bureaus must be contacted to ensure that the information is properly distributed.

Mortgage Speak

The **Fair Credit Reporting Act** is legislation that provides a borrower with a free copy of his or her report should the borrower be denied credit, with assistance to correct invalid information.

A credit bureau can remove an entry if they can show it does not belong to you and there's not proof that it is yours. You'll notice in our credit report example that the last page lists all companies that have an entry on your report, with their name, address, and phone numbers. This makes the follow-up much easier than in the past.

If You Have No Credit

There are those who have not established traditional credit usage, such as installment loans or credit cards. Yet a large part of the mortgage underwriter's decision lies with the borrower's ability to pay his or her monthly obligations. And some loan programs require a minimum of three or four active trade lines on a report before even considering the borrower. If a credit report is pulled and there are no trade lines (entries from creditors), or not enough trade lines exist, then an alternative credit report can be created.

Typically, credit card companies and loan institutions report regularly to the credit bureaus. But in the case of someone who doesn't have cards and loans, rent verification from a landlord, or utility payments for gas electric and telephone can be added.

The borrower should contact the respective company and ask for a payment-history letter. The letter will state the client's name, the type of account, and the payment history or quality of payment, for example, "Pays as agreed." The lender will provide the data to the credit bureau on behalf of the borrower, and the credit report will be created. Subprime loans may not be available to the client who has no credit history.

Resolving Poor Credit

Credit is a big part of the loan-approval process, and if debt is not paid as agreed, credit ratings drop. One or two slow pays typically require a brief explanation. But as more payments are missed, the overall credit becomes tarnished. To obtain a loan with the best interest rates, debts should be paid as agreed for a minimum of 12 to 18 months.

If you know you have a credit issue, address it, because the problem will not disappear on its own. The longer an account remains unresolved, additional costs may be incurred. The account may be transferred between different entities and it then become more difficult to settle as time goes on. Most creditors want a resolution. They are willing to work through the terms with you.

And the lender should be able to offer suggestions. After all, you're not the first, nor will you be the last, to have a few bruises. The great news is that credit issues can be resolved and tucked away as only a memory. If in the meantime you want or need to purchase a home, financing may be available.

Understanding Your Credit Score

A credit-scoring standard has been implemented in the mortgage loan decision-making process. The scores range from 300 to 900, with 900 being a superior rating. The credit score mathematically evaluates what type of a credit risk you may be by looking at several aspects of your credit. There is no guarantee that past performance will hold true in the future, but it's the lender's best way to determine credit worthiness.

The credit score takes into account the amount of open and available credit, how much outstanding debt you have, and how much may be available to you. The statistics also track how well you pay your monthly obligations, how long you've had credit, and how recently you have taken on new debt. Your mix of installment vs. revolving debt will also influence the score.

The reason the credit score is important to you is that many loan institutions offer abbreviated underwriting standards for credit scores above 720. If you find your credit score is below 620, there is cause for concern. Determine what is influencing the score. Lots of factors may influence where your score falls. Common reasons that a score may not be as high as you would hope are not paying on time, outstanding collections, high outstanding credit limits on revolving cards, and serious credit disturbances such as judgments, tax liens, or bankruptcy.

In some cases, there is a single account that has gone undetected for an extended period of time. Or your credit may not be mature enough to rebound on its own. Remember, the credit-scoring process reviews your history, and, as time passes and good credit is re-established, the averaging process is extended, hence enabling your score to rise. The scoring process is based upon decades of credit usage, and it may just be a matter of timing.

The credit score can be influenced by the number of times a credit report is reviewed, so it's a good practice to limit the amount of exposure you allow your credit. Particularly harmful is a trip to the car dealership, for example, where the salesperson is trying to be helpful and find the best financing solution for that sporty new car. Each creditor will typically want to look at their own version of credit, and it's easy to rack up four or five pulls within a 24-hour period. The computer notes the inquiries as a new concentrated spur of activity, and that's noted as derogatory. The credit score will be ratcheted downward.

Once you've determined what's on your report, immediately take steps to correct it. If you're behind on your credit card, be proactive and make arrangements with the creditor. Although it's an unpleasant call to make, they are more likely to work with you if you contact them rather than let them contact you.

And although the credit-scoring process may be a tool to help lenders evaluate you as a credit risk, they are not legally obligated to share the score with you. Most will give you the information as a courtesy, however.

Bet You Didn't Know

Each credit-reporting service has its own name for its score: TransUnion is called "empirica," Experian "fair issac" or "fico," and Equifax is known as a "beacon" score. These scores, or numbers, are those that an underwriter will use to help make a determination on your credit worthiness.

Bankruptcy

A bankruptcy suggests serious credit issues. There are two common types of bankruptcy: Chapter 7—all debt written off, and Chapter 13—debt is repaid, on a schedule set up through a court-appointed trustee. The creditors are asked to take an abbreviated settlement, but the client has agreed to pay back a large portion of the indebtedness, over a two- to five-year period. Your conscience and your attorney will help you to decide which is best for you. The lender always prefers to see that you've filed the Chapter 13, which shows you honored your obligations to your creditors. That doesn't forgive you for the credit mishap, but shows your intent to correct the problem.

For conforming loans, the bankruptcy needs to have been settled, or discharged a minimum of three to five years, depending on loan type. There are exceptions to every rule in financing, it seems. In this case, *if* the bankruptcy was the result of a catastrophic event, such as the death of the primary wager earner, or insurmountable medical debt due to illness, the waiting period may be shortened.

Also, the borrower must be able to show that credit has been re-established. New credit needs to be paid as agreed. So don't let yourself avoid credit after a bankruptcy. Embrace the bankruptcy as a learning experience and apply for a secured loan or a debit card tied to a bank account. You're not encouraged to go back into debt, but rather to show that you are capable of repaying an obligation in a timely fashion.

Bankruptcy, although a serious credit concern, need not be considered an insurmountable obstacle when borrowing. The subprime lending industry has evolved to meet this demand. You may still be eligible for a loan but the rate will be higher. Consider the opportunity if you can agree on the payment and terms. These loans can also help you quickly reestablish credit. There's nothing that says that, in a year or two, you won't be back on your feet and ready to refinance to a lower interest rate conforming loan. Chapter 10 is devoted to refinances.

Credit Counseling

Many consumers have turned to credit-counseling companies for guidance when trying to handle their debt. Some of these services have changed the lives of consumers in a very positive way. Good counselors and legitimate companies help to establish budgets and educate clients on money management. Many have programs in place where you make a lump-sum payment to the service, and they in turn distribute it amongst your creditors. The service may even be able to negotiate a settlement, based upon a guaranteed payback.

But a credit counselor cannot do anything that you cannot do on your own for significantly less money. And when you're preparing for a home purchase, it's important to understand how a mortgage lender views these credit counselors. You may have contracted with one of these companies because you're trying to be proactive and "manage" your money. If your payment history is good, then the mortgage lender may ask for a letter from the plan administrator indicating that they know you're contemplating a home purchase and that they give their approval. Usually, the letter must state you've participated in the program for a minimum of 12 months.

If you were having difficulty paying your debts and contracted with one of these organizations, then the process is viewed more like a Chapter 7 bankruptcy, and you may be required to pay through the entire program and wait a couple of years to purchase.

From the lender's viewpoint, if you felt the need to contact and contract with this type of organization, your credit position warrants a let's-wait-and-see attitude, hence at least 12 months. And although you were proactive in your money management, it may still influence your lender's decision and loan program.

Bet You Didn't Know

Not all credit-counseling companies have the consumer's best interests at heart. Many "counselors" are in fact salesmen and saleswomen representing debt consolidation companies, selling a high-interest-rate loan. Some companies make claims such as their ability to remove all derogatory credit legitimately. You might worry about a company that feels the need to tell you they are legitimate. Ask for references and consult with your own creditors to see if they have worked well with them in the past.

Alternative Solution Financing

The mortgage industry is very astute when it comes to creating lending solutions that meet consumer needs. As debt in our society has risen, so have the incidents of slow payments. So they have created a new level of financing criteria that take into consideration the risks at this new level. We've also mentioned that as the risk has gone up, so has the cost of doing business, both in closing costs and rate.

The higher rate shouldn't be construed as a bad thing. It's not been too long ago that if you had walked into the lender with no income showing on your 1040, your options would have been nil to none. The lender would have told you to go home until you had a valid two years on your tax return. Even if the rate is higher, you have a mortgage interest deduction. And if your taxable income is lower, it could be a positive opportunity.

Just because you choose to finance this way now doesn't mean you're tied into the loan forever. The idea behind alternative financing is to give you an option today if you need to or want to buy. But as your circumstances improve over the next 18 to 24 months, by all means you should consider refinancing for better terms. Make certain that you've investigated the question of pre-payment and any penalties, particularly on the alternative loans.

To recap, alternative solutions enable you to bypass traditional qualification methods. You may elect to try one of the following loans if you cannot provide

documentation as needed, or if your credit circumstances warrant. The common loan products available are these:

- **Stated income/stated asset.** The lender will
  use the numbers you provide to them on the
  application and will not verify them in the
  traditional method, i.e., with paystubs or tax
  returns.

- **No income verification/no asset verification.** The lender will not complete any
  information regarding income and assets on
  the application.

- **No documentation loans.** The lender will
  rely on their credit report, without any asset
  or income verification.

- **No down payment loans.** Usually for borrowers who are asset challenged; there are a
  few loans that truly allow 100% financing,
  either a community resource loan product or
  as a first and second mortgage combination.

- **Down Payment Assistance loans.** Allow
  you to borrow funds from a nonprofit organization and the loan may be either when the
  home is sold or after a specified length of
  time for ownership.

Your own personal financial circumstances will dictate the loans that you'll be interested in. And if you
don't necessarily fit the model for the conforming
loans, there are a variety of other solutions.

The Least You Need to Know

- It's okay to have circumstances outside of the box; there are still financing solutions available.

- Subprime lending has provided loan solutions for those with substandard credit histories as well as those borrowers who may not fit the conforming loan mold.

- Your credit score is influenced by the amount of credit and the combination of installment and revolving accounts, as well as how timely you are at repayment.

- If you have incorrect entries on your credit report, the reporting bureau is required to assist you in correcting information because of the Fair Credit Reporting Act; you also have a right to review your credit if for any reason you are denied credit.

Chapter 5

Understanding the Costs of Doing Business

In This Chapter

- Getting an estimate of the costs
- Itemizing the financed amount
- Learning the truth about the APR

It's been said that the only thing a lender does not ask for at the loan application is your blood type. Yet if you were lending your money to a perfect stranger, you would definitely want to know that it was likely the loan could and would be repaid. The series of application questions and the list of documents needed are simply the easiest way for a lender to get to know a prospective borrower and determine if he is a good candidate for a loan.

But after the interview is completed and you've handed over your paperwork, the lender is going to provide you with several documents that will explain and define the terms and conditions of the loan you've just applied for. Now it's your turn to ask the questions; this chapter will help you to educate yourself on what to expect from the lender and how to read those documents and disclosures.

You will find that there are differences between all lenders in their approaches, their costs, and their products. Fortunately, there are government disclosure laws in place that require all lenders to provide the same information in similar format, making it easier to make comparisons. This is helpful especially when trying to determine the cost to do business.

Good Faith Estimate

In Chapter 1, we discussed the question "How much home can you afford?" When you meet with a lender and fill out a Uniform Residential Loan Application (remember that from Chapter 3?), they are required to provide an estimate of fees associated with obtaining a home loan, along with a reasonable estimate of the payment.

The estimate includes a breakdown of the mortgage payment showing property taxes, homeowner's insurance, and mortgage insurance, if applicable. Mortgage insurance may be required on certain loan types, and is fully explained in Chapter 6. The sales price, down payment, and loan amount are shown, along with the loan-product term and interest rate. Fees are listed in categories, by lender and closing/escrow company.

> ## Bet You Didn't Know
>
> Escrow can have two meanings in the mortgage industry, but both refer to holding money: First, an "escrow account" means to impound (with the lender) the monies necessary to pay for property taxes and any insurance required for the loan. The "escrow closing" refers to a third party that holds all earnest/security deposits, pending satisfaction of all closing contingencies. They are also responsible for acting on behalf of the lender, facilitating deed transfers.

The form, known as a *Good Faith Estimate of Settlement Costs*, means that in "good faith" the lender will provide you with figures based upon the information as it is known today; sales price (or proposed sales price in the case of a pre-approval), loan amount, and customary fees for your locale. Most likely, no two lender good faith estimates will look alike and no two companies will list their fees the same. But an overall comparison can be made because there are line-item entry similarities mandated by the federal government.

GOOD FAITH ESTIMATE

Applicants: John Doe / Jane Doe
Property Addr: 123 Pleasantville, Anywhere, USA,

Application No: 31112003
Date Prepared: 01/29/2003
Loan Program: 30 YEAR FIXED

The information provided below reflects estimates of the charges which you are likely to incur at the settlement of your loan. The fees listed are estimates–actual charges may be more or less. Your transaction may not involve a fee for every item listed. The numbers listed beside the estimates generally correspond to the numbered lines contained in the HUD-1 settlement statement which you will be receiving at settlement. The HUD-1 settlement statement will show you the actual cost for items paid at settlement.

Total Loan Amount $ 145,400   Interest Rate: 6.000 %   Term: 360 / 360 mths

800	ITEMS PAYABLE IN CONNECTION WITH LOAN:			
801	Loan Origination Fee		$	
802	Loan Discount			
803	Appraisal Fee		300.00	
804	Credit Report		50.00	
805	Lender's Inspection Fee			
808	Mortgage Broker Fee			
809	Tax Related Service Fee		80.00	PFC
810	Processing Fee		250.00	PFC
811	Underwriting Fee		350.00	PFC
812	Wire Transfer Fee			
	FLOOD LIFE OF LOAN CERTIFICATE		16.00	PFC
	COURIER FEE		20.00	PFC
				PFC
				PFC

1100	TITLE CHARGES:			
1101	Closing or Escrow Fee:		$ 185.00	
1105	Document Preparation Fee			
1106	Notary Fees			
1107	Attorney Fees			
1108	Title Insurance:		525.00	
	TITLE ENDORSEMENTS- EPA & SURVEY		200.00	
	TITLE BINDER		50.00	

1200	GOVERNMENT RECORDING & TRANSFER CHARGES:			
1201	Recording Fees:		$ 70.00	
1202	City/County Tax/Stamps:			
1203	State Tax/Stamps:			
	ASSIGNMENT		16.00	PFC

1300	ADDITIONAL SETTLEMENT CHARGES:			
1302	Pest Inspection		$	
	SURVEY		140.00	

		Estimated Closing Costs	2,252.00	

900	ITEMS REQUIRED BY LENDER TO BE PAID IN ADVANCE:			
901	Interest for 15 days @ $ 23.9014 per day		$ 358.52	PFC
902	Mortgage Insurance Premium			
903	Hazard Insurance Premium		480.00	PFC
904				
905	VA Funding Fee			PFC

1000	RESERVES DEPOSITED WITH LENDER:			
1001	Hazard Insurance Premiums	2 months @ $ 40.00 per month	$ 80.00	
1002	Mortgage Ins. Premium Reserves	months @ $ 65.00 per month		PFC
1003	School Tax	months @ $ per month		
1004	Taxes and Assessment Reserves	2 months @ $ 200.00 per month	400.00	
1005	Flood Insurance Reserves	months @ $ per month		
		months @ $ per month		
		months @ $ per month		

		Estimated Prepaid Items/Reserves	1,318.52	
TOTAL ESTIMATED SETTLEMENT CHARGES			3,570.52	

TOTAL ESTIMATED FUNDS NEEDED TO CLOSE:				
Purchase Price/Payoff (+)	161,500.00		Principal & Interest	871.75
Loan Amount (-)	145,400.00		Other Financing (P & I)	0.00
Est. Closing Costs (+)	2,252.00		Hazard Insurance	40.00
Est Prepaid Items/Reserves (+)	1,318.52		Real Estate Taxes	200.00
Amount Paid by Seller (-)			Homeowner Insurance	65.00
			Homeowner Assn. Dues	
			Other	
Total Est. Funds needed to close	19,770.52		Total Monthly Payment	1,176.75

These estimates are provided pursuant to the Real Estate Settlement Procedures Act of 1974, as amended (RESPA). Additional information can be found in the HUD Special Information Booklet, which is to be provided to you by your mortgage broker or lender. If your application is to purchase residential real property and the lender will take a first lien on the property. The undersigned acknowledges receipt of the booklet "Settlement Costs," and if applicable the Consumer Handbook on ARM Mortgages.

Applicant John Doe _____ Date _____   Applicant Jane Doe _____ Date _____

Good Faith Estimate.

GOOD FAITH ESTIMATE

Applicants: John Doe / Jane Doe
Property Addr: 123 Pleasantville, Anywhere, USA,

Application No: 31112003
Date Prepared: 01/29/2003
Loan Program: 30 YEAR FIXED

The information provided below reflects estimates of the charges which you are likely to incur at the settlement of your loan. The fees listed are estimates-actual charges may be more or less. Your transaction may not involve a fee for every item listed. The numbers listed beside the estimates generally correspond to the numbered lines contained in the HUD-1 settlement statement which you will be receiving at settlement. The HUD-1 settlement statement will show you the actual cost for items paid at settlement.

Total Loan Amount $ 145,400   Interest Rate: 6.000 %   Term: 360 / 360 mths

800	ITEMS PAYABLE IN CONNECTION WITH LOAN:	$	
801	Loan Origination Fee		
802	Loan Discount		
803	Appraisal Fee	300.00	
804	Credit Report	50.00	
805	Lender's Inspection Fee		
808	Mortgage Broker Fee		
809	Tax Related Service Fee	80.00	PFC
810	Processing Fee	250.00	PFC
811	Underwriting Fee	350.00	PFC
812	Wire Transfer Fee		
	FLOOD LIFE OF LOAN CERTIFICATE	16.00	PFC
	COURIER FEE	20.00	PFC
			PFC
			PFC

Line Items 800 through 812.

Items in section 800 cover the lender charges.

Item 801 is the lender's fee to do the loan.

Item 802 lists any discount points, which are the costs associated with obtaining the interest rate (see Chapter 8).

Item 803 is the appraisal fee, which is often collected at the beginning of the transaction as an application fee.

Item 804 is the credit report fee, which is often collected at the beginning of the transaction as an application fee.

Item 805 is the lender's inspection fee. If there is any type of work that requires completion prior to closing, the lender may send out an inspector to verify completion.

Item 808 is the mortgage broker fee, which is a fee charged by a broker that represents their yield spread, or gross income.

Item 809 is the tax-related service fee. Because most mortgage lenders require taxes to be paid as part of the payment, separate companies now work on contract with lenders to search tax bills at county tax assessors' offices to ensure that taxes are properly credited when paid. This is the fee for that service.

Item 810 is the processing fee, which a lender can charge for administering loan documentation and collecting necessary information.

Item 811 is the underwriting fee, which the lender can charge for assessing the credit risk associated with a mortgage loan.

Item 812 is a wire transfer fee, which is a cost associated with electronically transferring money from bank to bank rather than by check.

The Flood Life of Loan Certification fee determines if a property lies within a flood plain. If it does not, the flood determination company certifies and warrants that the property does not lie within a flood plain for the life of the loan.

The Courier Fee is for express mail/overnight mail.

Items in section 1100 are estimates of fees that are actually provided by the title company so that the borrower has an accurate estimate of monies needed to be brought to closing.

Item 1101 is the closing agent's fee for administering the paperwork at closing.

Item 1105 is the document preparation fee for preparation of legal mortgage documents.

Item 1106 is the notary fees for a Notary Public to acknowledge signatures.

Item 1107 is the attorney fees for a closing attorney review.

Item 1108 is affirmative insurance coverage to ensure the lender's priority lien position and to guarantee to the owner that they have marketable title to the property.

The Title Endorsements—EPA & Survey insures the lender against the loss in marketability of the title due to hazardous environmental conditions.

1100	TITLE CHARGES:		
1101	Closing or Escrow Fee:	$	185.00
1105	Document Preparation Fee		
1106	Notary Fees		
1107	Attorney Fees		
1108	Title Insurance:		525.00
	TITLE ENDORSEMENTS- EPA & SURVEY		200.00
	TITLE BINDER		60.00

1200	GOVERNMENT RECORDING & TRANSFER CHARGES:		
1201	Recording Fees:	$	70.00
1202	City/County Tax/Stamps:		
1203	State Tax/Stamps:		
	ASSIGNMENT		16.00 PFC

1300	ADDITIONAL SETTLEMENT CHARGES:		
1302	Pest Inspection	$	
	SURVEY		140.00

| | *Estimated Closing Costs* | | 2,252.00 |

Line Items 1100 through 1302.

The Title Binder shows the proposed insured (i.e., lender and owner), the legal names under which they will take title, the amounts of coverage, the terms under which the proposed policy will be issued, and the expiration date of the binder.

Items in section 1200 are the government recording and transfer charge fees charged by municipalities for recording documents for public records.

Item 1201 is the recording fee charged by the county recorder or clerk to make a document a matter of public record.

Item 1202 is for the city and county tax stamps.

Item 1203 is a transaction fee charged by some states when a property is conveyed or encumbered with a lien.

The Assignment fee is collected at the time of closing to process and record an assignment of rights to the mortgage from one lender to another.

Items in section 1300 are any additional settlement charges.

Item 1302 is any fees charged by a pest control firm to determine if there is evidence of insect infestation or dry rot.

The Survey is a schematic description of where the house lies in relationship to property boundaries.

900	ITEMS REQUIRED BY LENDER TO BE PAID IN ADVANCE:				
901	Interest for 15 days @ $ 23.9014 per day		$	358.52	PFC
902	Mortgage Insurance Premium				
903	Hazard Insurance Premium			480.00	PFC
904					
905	VA Funding Fee				PFC
1000	RESERVES DEPOSITED WITH LENDER:				
1001	Hazard Insurance Premiums	2 months @ $ 40.00 per month	$	80.00	
1002	Mortgage Ins. Premium Reserves	months @ $ 65.00 per month			PFC
1003	School Tax	months @ $ per month			
1004	Taxes and Assessment Reserves	2 months @ $ 200.00 per month		400.00	
1005	Flood Insurance Reserves	months @ $ per month			
		months @ $ per month			
		months @ $ per month			
		Estimated Prepaid Items/Reserves		1,318.52	
TOTAL ESTIMATED SETTLEMENT CHARGES				3,570.52	

Line Items 900 to the TOTAL ESTIMATED SETTLEMENT CHARGES.

Items in section 900 are required to be set aside for the prepaid expenses of taxes, insurances, and interest, as described in Chapter 3. At closing you will be required to impound enough of each to make certain that as taxes and insurance come due, money is available to pay them.

Item 901 is the $XX.XX amount of interest per day you are responsible for from the date of closing through the remainder of the month in which you close.

Item 902 is the Mortgage Insurance Premium, which is the risk insurance paid on behalf of the lender by borrowers with lower down payments.

Item 903 is the hazard insurance premiums paid in advance of its use; therefore, 1 year is required paid at closing by the borrower.

Item 905 is the VA's funding fee to administer their loan.

Items in section 1000 are for the escrow account. Monies are not set aside in this account arbitrarily; only funds needed can be escrowed to pay future installments of taxes and insurance, enforced by federal legislation. These funds are held in non-interest-bearing trust accounts on behalf of the borrower.

Item 1001 is the hazard insurance premium, which is set aside if there is an impound, or perhaps a condo fee that will be reconciled at closing, but is not part of the actual escrow.

Item 1002 is the Mortgage Insurance Premium reserves, which is the risk insurance escrow impound.

Items 1003, 1004, and 1005 are covered in more detail in Chapter 3.

The TOTAL ESTIMATED SETTLEMENT CHARGES are added up.

The section on the TOTAL ESTIMATED FUNDS NEEDED TO CLOSE is described as follows:

- Purchase Price/Payoff (+) is the price paid for the house; the balance of mortgage for refinance.

- Loan Amount (–) is the amount borrowed.

- Est. Closing Costs (+) are the fees to close from both the lender and the closing agent.

- Est. Prepaid Items/Reserves (+) are the escrow impounds and prepaid interest through the end of the month in which you close.

- Amount Paid by Seller (–) is the cash the seller has agreed contractually to contribute toward the buyer's expenses to close.

- Total Estimated Funds Needed to Close is the money to bring to the closing (either cashier's check or wired).

TOTAL ESTIMATED FUNDS NEEDED TO CLOSE:

Purchase Price/Payoff (+)	161,600.00	Principal & Interest	871.75
Loan Amount (-)	145,400.00	Other Financing (P & I)	0.00
Est. Closing Costs (+)	2,252.00	Hazard Insurance	40.00
Est. Prepaid Items/Reserves (+)	1,318.52	Real Estate Taxes	200.00
Amount Paid by Seller (-)		Mortgage Insurance	65.00
		Homeowner Assn. Dues	
		Other	
Total Est. Funds needed to close	**19,770.52**	**Total Monthly Payment**	**1,176.75**

These estimates are provided pursuant to the Real Estate Settlement Procedures Act of 1974, as amended (RESPA). Additional information can be found in the HUD Special Information Booklet, which is to be provided to you by your mortgage broker or lender, if your application is to purchase residential real property and the lender will take a first lien on the property. The undersigned acknowledges receipt of the booklet "Settlement Costs," and if applicable the Consumer Handbook on ARM Mortgages.

Applicant John Doe	Date	Applicant Jane Doe	Date

TOTAL ESTIMATED FUNDS NEEDED TO CLOSE to signatures.

The section on the TOTAL ESTIMATED MONTHLY PAYMENT is described as follows:

- Principal & Interest is the amortized monthly payment representing both principal and interest.

- Other Financing (P & I) is any second mortgage included as described in Chapter 8.

- Hazard Insurance is the annual hazard insurance premium divided by 12.

- Real Estate Taxes are the annual property taxes divided by 12.

- Mortgage Insurance is the annual mortgage insurance premium divided by 12.

- Homeowner Association Dues are paid to the association, not the lender, but are included in the total monthly housing expense for qualification purposes.

- Anything listed under Other may include special assessments for sewer, paving, sidewalks, recreation districts, etc.

- Total Monthly Payment is the amount you can expect to pay each month to your lender.

There are several standard expenses when you take out a mortgage loan, and I'll discuss the closing costs you may expect to pay in Chapter 9, when we review the *HUD-1 Settlement Statement*. But there may be fees charged that represent direct profit to the lender. Unscrupulous lenders may attempt to "pad" the good faith estimate with so-called "junk fees." These fees may appear as normal fees at in-flated rates, or may be altogether bogus. And when comparing programs and fees, you'll find that the descriptions may vary, making it difficult to compare. This is why the good faith estimate and its standard format is so important.

Mortgage Speak

The HUD-1 Settlement Statement, also known as the Closing Statement in Chapter 9, is the document prepared that reconciles the settlement fees for both borrowers and sellers at closing.

Truth in Lending Disclosure Statement

Anytime you borrow money, whether it is for a home or auto loan, or even for a credit card, the lender is required by law to provide you a summary of the cost of obtaining credit. Known as a *Truth in Lending Disclosure*, this standard form reiterates to the consumer that there are costs associated with borrowing money. This disclosure also points out the terms of the loan and any peculiarities to the loan, such as a prepayment penalty or a due-on-sale clause.

TRUTH-IN-LENDING DISCLOSURE STATEMENT
(THIS IS NEITHER A CONTRACT NOR A COMMITMENT TO LEND)

Applicants: John Doe
Jane Doe

Property Address: 123 Pleasantville
Anywhere, USA,

Application No: 31112003

Date Prepared: 01/29/2003

ANNUAL PERCENTAGE RATE	FINANCE CHARGE	AMOUNT FINANCED	TOTAL OF PAYMENTS
The cost of your credit as a yearly rate	The dollar amount the credit will cost you	The amount of credit provided to you or on your behalf	The amount you will have paid after making all payments as scheduled
* 6.420 %	$ * 176,691.86	$ * 143,829.48	$ * 320,521.34

☐ REQUIRED DEPOSIT: The annual percentage rate does not take into account your required deposit
PAYMENTS: Your payment schedule will be:

Number of Payments	Amount of Payments **	When Payments Are Due	Number of Payments	Amount of Payments **	When Payments Are Due	Number of Payments	Amount of Payments **	When Payments Are Due
		Monthly Beginning:			Monthly Beginning:			Monthly Beginning:
103	936.75	06/01/2003						
256	871.75	01/01/2012						
1	868.09	05/01/2033						

☐ DEMAND FEATURE: This obligation has a demand feature.
☐ VARIABLE RATE FEATURE: This loan contains a variable rate feature. A variable rate disclosure has been provided earlier.

CREDIT LIFE/CREDIT DISABILITY: Credit life insurance and credit disability insurance are not required to obtain credit, and will not be provided unless you sign and agree to pay the additional cost.

Type	Premium	Signature	
Credit Life		I want credit life insurance.	Signature:
Credit Disability		I want credit disability insurance.	Signature:
Credit Life and Disability		I want credit life and disability insurance.	Signature:

INSURANCE: The following insurance is required to obtain credit:
☐ Credit life insurance ☐ Credit disability ☑ Property insurance ☐ Flood insurance
You may obtain the insurance from anyone you want that is acceptable to creditor
☐ If you purchase ☐ property ☐ flood insurance from creditor you will pay $ for a one year term.
SECURITY: You are giving a security interest in:
☑ The goods or property being purchased ☐ Real property you already own.
FILING FEES: $ 55.00
LATE CHARGE: If a payment is more than 15 days late, you will be charged 5.000 % of the payment
PREPAYMENT: If you pay off early, you
☐ may ☑ will not have to pay a penalty.
☐ may ☑ will not be entitled to a refund of part of the finance charge.
ASSUMPTION: Someone buying your property
☐ may ☐ may, subject to conditions ☐ may not assume the remainder of your loan on the original terms.
See your contract documents for any additional information about nonpayment, default, any required repayment in full before the scheduled date and prepayment refunds and penalties
☑ * means an estimate ☑ all dates and numerical disclosures except the late payment disclosures are estimates.
* * NOTE: The Payments shown above include reserve deposits for Mortgage Insurance (if applicable), but exclude Property Taxes and Insurance.

THE UNDERSIGNED ACKNOWLEDGES RECEIVING A COMPLETED COPY OF THIS DISCLOSURE.

John Doe	(Applicant)	(Date)	Jane Doe	(Applicant)	(Date)
	(Applicant)	(Date)		(Applicant)	(Date)
	(Lender)	(Date)			

Truth-in-Lending Disclosure Statement.

The Truth in Lending is helpful because it includes the following calculations (in boxes at the top of the document):

- Annual Percentage Rate
- Finance Charge
- Amount Financed
- Total of Payments

The *Annual Percentage Rate* (*APR*) calculation is determined by taking the interest rate and adding in the finance charges that the lender will collect over the life of the loan.

Mortgage Speak

The **Annual Percentage Rate (APR)** is a required federal calculation that shows the cost of the mortgage yearly, based upon fees paid to obtain the loan. The APR is usually higher than the actual interest rate, and is used by borrowers to compare lender's fees.

A "good deal" is when the interest rate and the annual percentage rate are close, e.g., 6.0 and 6.42, as in our example document. This means that you are not paying excess loan fees. The APR will rise if closing fees are high. Note that on the Good Faith Estimate the fees marked with PFC (prepaid finance charge) indicate those fees considered in the APR calculation.

The Finance Charge indicates the amount of interest you will pay to obtain the loan. This figure of $176,691.86 assumes that you will make every payment as agreed and will not make early prepayments to the principal. If you do pay extra principal during the life of the loan, the finance charge amount will ultimately be not as high.

The Amount Financed is the loan amount of $145,400 less the prepaid finance charges of $1570.52, $143,829.48. You are actually borrowing the entire amount, but the government requires the lender to reflect the amounts independently, again to show the cost of doing the loan.

Finally, the Total of Payments is calculated by adding the Finance Charge and Amount Financed. If you were to prepay toward the loan principal at any time, the total would be lower (because you didn't pay as much in finance charges). You only pay interest on those monies you use for the period of time you keep them.

Itemization of Amount Financed

The annual percentage rate calculation was created to promote awareness and protect consumers from outlandish fees. Yet to most who borrow money, it makes no sense. The following *Itemization of Amount Financed* document helps to explain what fees are included in the APR calculation.

ITEMIZATION OF AMOUNT FINANCED

Applicants:	John Doe
	Jane Doe
Property Addr:	123 Pleasantville
	Anywhere, USA,
Application No:	31112003

Date Prepared: 01/29/2003

Total Loan Amount $	145,400.00	Prepaid Finance Charge $	1,570.52	Amount Financed $	143,829.48

ITEMIZATION OF PREPAID FINANCE CHARGE

Tax Related Service Fee			80.00
Processing Fee			250.00
Underwriting Fee			350.00
FLOOD LIFE OF LOAN CERTIFICATE			16.00
COURIER FEE			20.00
Interest for	15 days @ $	23.9014 per day	358.52
Hazard Insurance Premium			480.00
VA Funding Fee			
Mortgage Ins. Premium Reserves		65.00 per month	
ASSIGNMENT			16.00
Total Prepaid Finance Charge			1,570.52

AMOUNT PAID ON YOUR ACCOUNT / PAID TO OTHERS ON YOUR BEHALF

Loan Origination Fee			
Loan Discount			
Appraisal Fee			300.00
Credit Report			50.00
Lender's Inspection Fee			
Mortgage Broker Fee			
Wire Transfer Fee			
Mortgage Insurance Premium			
Hazard Insurance Premiums	2 months @ $	40.00 per month	80.00
School Tax			
Taxes and Assessment Reserves	2 months @ $	200.00 per month	400.00
Flood Insurance Reserves			
Closing or Escrow Fee:			185.00
Document Preparation Fee			
Notary Fees			
Attorney Fees			
Title Insurance:			525.00
TITLE ENDORSEMENTS- EPA & SURVEY			200.00
TITLE BINDER			50.00
Recording Fees:			70.00
City/County Tax/Stamps:			
State Tax/Stamps			
Pest Inspection			
SURVEY			140.00
Total Estimated Settlement Charge			3,570.52

Applicant John Doe	Date	Applicant Jane Doe	Date

Itemization of Amount Financed.

ITEMIZATION OF AMOUNT FINANCED

Applicants:	John Doe
	Jane Doe
Property Addr:	123 Pleasantville
	Anywhere, USA,
Application No:	31112003

Date Prepared: 01/29/2003

| Total Loan Amount $ | 145,400.00 | Prepaid Finance Charge $ | 1,570.52 | Amount Financed $ | 143,829.48 |

ITEMIZATION OF PREPAID FINANCE CHARGE

Tax Related Service Fee	80.00
Processing Fee	250.00
Underwriting Fee	350.00
FLOOD LIFE OF LOAN CERTIFICATE	16.00
COURIER FEE	20.00
Interest for 15 days @ $ 23.9014 per day	358.52
Hazard Insurance Premium	480.00
VA Funding Fee	
Mortgage Ins. Premium Reserves 65.00 per month	
ASSIGNMENT	16.00
Total Prepaid Finance Charge	1,570.52

Itemization of Prepaid Finance Charge.

AMOUNT PAID ON YOUR ACCOUNT / PAID TO OTHERS ON YOUR BEHALF		
Loan Origination Fee		
Loan Discount		
Appraisal Fee		300.00
Credit Report		50.00
Lender's Inspection Fee		
Mortgage Broker Fee		
Wire Transfer Fee		
Mortgage Insurance Premium		
Hazard Insurance Preminums	2 months @ $ 40.00 per month	80.00
School Tax		
Taxes and Assessment Reserves	2 months @ $ 200.00 per month	400.00
Flood Insurance Reserves		

Amount Paid on Your Account / Paid to Others on Your Behalf (part 1).

Closing or Escrow Fee:	185.00
Document Preparation Fee	
Notary Fees	
Attorney Fees	
Title Insurance:	
TITLE ENDORSEMENTS- EPA & SURVEY	525.00
	200.00
TITLE BINDER	50.00
Recording Fees:	
City/County Tax/Stamps:	70.00
State Tax/Stamps	
Pest Inspection	
SURVEY	140.00
Total Estimated Settlement Charge	3,570.52

Amount Paid on Your Account / Paid to Others on Your Behalf (part 2).

Prepaid finance expenses have been defined as costs the borrower must pay to actually obtain the loan (not to be confused with "closing on the loan"). The federal government wanted to make certain that borrowers were aware of what fees they were paying to actually get a mortgage, and by creating this calculation, there was the opportunity to compare fees with the rate directly.

It's Your Money

You might notice that "Assignment" (listed after Line Item 1002 on the *Itemization of Amount Financed* document) is not anywhere on the *Good Faith Estimate*. This fee might be incurred when the lender is transferring the loan to another institution, such as a broker. The fee is most likely lumped into a recording fee on the *Good Faith Estimate*.

The Least You Need to Know

- The Good Faith Estimate and Truth in Lending disclosures are both provided to inform the borrower of the costs to obtain credit.
- Fees will vary from lender to lender, but you can compare based upon the categories established on the Good Faith Estimate.

- The Closing/Settlement Statement in Chapter 10 correlates with the Good Faith Estimate as a cross reference.

- The Annual Percentage Rate (APR) is not the rate of interest your payment is calculated at, but rather the annualized rate if all prepaid finance charge expenses are included in the rate.

Chapter 6

Choosing the Best Type of Loan

In This Chapter

- The repayment system called amortization
- How pre-payment options work
- What mortgage insurance is and why you need it

When it comes to borrowing money to purchase your home, fear not. There is a solution for everyone, if you're talking to the right lender. Remember, not everybody's financial circumstances are the same. Today, there is an unprecedented variety of loan products and programs available, each priced relative to the amount of risk the lender is absorbing for the transaction. No longer is homeownership for only those with picture-perfect credit and "lifers" in their occupations. The mortgage-lending industry continues to develop innovative solutions to meet the ever-changing needs of the buyer.

How Mortgage Loans Are Repaid: Amortization

As you explore home financing, it's important to understand the mechanics of how mortgage loans are repaid. When a payment is made, there are not equal amounts of principal and interest repaid monthly. A complex repayment process known as *amortization* is done on home loans. On a regular mortgage loan, interest is front-loaded. That's to say that when you're paying back the loan, the first several years you're actually repaying a lot of the interest on the money and a little bit of the principal amount you borrowed. The lender gets their money they lent to you returned faster than you build the equity, or savings, in the home.

 **Mortgage Speak**

Amortization is the repayment of a liability with a portion of the payment being applied toward the principal balance as well as toward the interest owed.

To illustrate, I've included a payment schedule for the first 36 months of a loan. The interest rate is 6.0 percent and the amount borrowed is $145,400. Each payment made is the same, at $936.75 (until payment #104). But notice how each monthly payment is divided. For example, payment 1 has

$144.75 going toward the principal. So after the first payment you now owe the lender $145,255.25. The remaining $792.00 is the interest that the lender will receive for lending you the money. Now, granted, the lender had to pay something for the money they have lent to you, and there are a lot of people who touch your file while you have this loan, so I'm not saying it's a bad thing. It is, however, very important that you realize where your payment is applied each month.

This amortization schedule in its entirety would reflect all 360 payments for this 30-year loan. As you continue down the partial schedule, the remaining balance continues to decrease. At the end of the thirty-sixth payment, you now owe the lender $139,706.10. You will have paid $2,012.63 toward the principal reduction, the lender will have received $25,689.10 in interest, and $2,340 was paid towards private mortgage insurance.

It's Your Money

As you look at the amortization table, you'll notice the interest expense going down over the years. This means that more of your payment is going to actually pay off the mortgage principal and build equity in your home. It also means that your interest expense and interest expense tax deduction is going down over the years.

Amortization Schedule

No.	Pmt. Date	Interest Rate	Payment	Monthly Payment Principal	Interest/MI	Remaining Balance
1	06/01/2003	6.000	936.75	144.75	792.00	145,255.25
2	07/01/2003	6.000	936.75	145.47	791.28	145,109.78
3	08/01/2003	6.000	936.75	146.20	790.55	144,963.58
4	09/01/2003	6.000	936.75	146.93	789.82	144,816.65
5	10/01/2003	6.000	936.75	147.67	789.08	144,668.98
6	11/01/2003	6.000	936.75	148.41	788.34	144,520.57
7	12/01/2003	6.000	936.75	149.15	787.60	144,371.42
YR 1			6,557.25	1,028.58	5,528.67	
8	01/01/2004	6.000	936.75	149.89	786.86	144,221.53
9	02/01/2004	6.000	936.75	150.64	786.11	144,070.89
10	03/01/2004	6.000	936.75	151.40	785.35	143,919.49

No.	Pmt. Date	Interest Rate	Payment	Monthly Payment Principal	Interest/MI	Remaining Balance
11	04/01/2004	6.000	936.75	152.15	784.60	143,767.34
12	05/01/2004	6.000	936.75	152.91	783.84	143,614.43
13	06/01/2004	6.000	936.75	153.68	783.07	143,460.75
14	07/01/2004	6.000	936.75	154.45	782.30	143,306.30
15	08/01/2004	6.000	936.75	155.22	781.53	143,151.08
16	09/01/2004	6.000	936.75	155.99	780.76	142,995.09
17	10/01/2004	6.000	936.75	156.77	779.98	142,838.32
18	11/01/2004	6.000	936.75	157.56	779.19	142,680.76
19	12/01/2004	6.000	936.75	158.35	778.40	142,522.41
YR 2			11,241.00	1,849.01	9,391.99	
20	01/01/2005	6.000	936.75	159.14	777.61	142,363.27
21	02/01/2005	6.000	936.75	159.93	776.82	142,203.34

continues

continued

No.	Pmt. Date	Interest Rate	Payment	Monthly Payment Principal	Interest/MI	Remaining Balance
22	03/01/2005	6.000	936.75	160.73	776.02	142,042.61
23	04/01/2005	6.000	936.75	161.54	775.21	141,881.07
24	05/01/2005	6.000	936.75	162.34	774.41	141,718.73
25	06/01/2005	6.000	936.75	163.16	773.59	141,555.57
26	07/01/2005	6.000	936.75	163.97	772.78	141,391.60
27	08/01/2005	6.000	936.75	164.79	771.96	141,226.81
28	09/01/2005	6.000	936.75	165.62	771.13	141,061.19
29	10/01/2005	6.000	936.75	166.44	770.31	140,894.75
30	11/01/2005	6.000	936.75	167.28	769.47	140,727.47
31	12/01/2005	6.000	936.75	168.11	768.64	140,559.36
YR 3			11,241.00	1,849.01	9,391.99	
32	01/01/2006	6.000	936.75	168.95	767.80	140,390.41

No.	Pmt. Date	Interest Rate	Payment	Monthly Payment Principal	Interest/MI	Remaining Balance
33	02/01/2006	6.000	936.75	169.80	766.95	140,220.61
34	03/01/2006	6.000	936.75	170.65	766.10	140,049.96
35	04/01/2006	6.000	936.75	171.50	765.25	139,878.46
36	05/01/2006	6.000	936.75	172.36	764.39	139,706.10
TOTAL after 36 months			33,723.00	2,012.36	28,029.10	
...						
103	12/01/2011	6.000	936.75	240.74	696.01	125,960.28
...						
104	01/01/2012	6.000	871.75	241.95	629.80	125,718.33
...						

continues

continued

No.	Pmt. Date	Interest Rate	Payment	Monthly Payment Principal	Interest/MI	Remaining Balance
356	01/01/2033	6.000	871.75	850.30	21.45	3,440.26
357	02/01/2033	6.000	871.75	854.55	17.20	2,585.71
358	03/01/2033	6.000	871.75	858.82	12.93	1,726.89
359	04/01/2033	6.000	871.75	863.12	8.63	863.77
360	05/01/2033	6.000	868.09	863.77	4.32	0.00
TOTAL			320,521.34	145,400.00	175,121.34	

Note: Mortgage insurance premiums, if paid monthly, may decrease over time; therefore, in approximately the tenth year, you may see the required monthly amount collected decrease.

This is how all mortgage amortization is structured. The variables are the interest rate, the amount borrowed, and the number of years you sign up to repay the loan.

Calculating Payments on Your Own Using Excel

The amortization tables at the back of the book are a handy way to quickly determine a payment for a mortgage loan you are considering. Another fun way to get exact information without using a table or calling up your mortgage broker is to use the Excel spreadsheet functions.

Let's do one together. Let's say you are considering a 30-year, 6 percent loan of $200,000, and you want to know how much your payment would change if you wait for rates to drop to 5 percent.

Using Microsoft Excel, your entries would be:

1. Click the f_x **Paste Function** button on the Standard toolbar.
2. Choose Function category: **Financial.**
3. Choose Function name: **PMT.**
4. Click **OK.**
5. Enter Rate: **.06/12** (.06 is the interest rate and 12 is to give you a monthly payment).
6. Enter NPER: **30*12** (360 for the number of months in 30 years of monthly payments; this would be 180 if only a 15-year loan).

7. Enter PV: **200000** (amount you want to finance).

8. Click **OK.**

The dialog box returns $1432.86. Notice that it is a negative number. This is a convention used in this type of financial calculation. If it bothers you, you can enter the amount of the loan as a negative number and the payment will read as a positive number.

Typing over the numbers in the Rate box to make it **.05/12** would change the result to $1319.91. This will allow you to compare your two interest rates. If you move down one cell you can save both calculations for later review.

As you play with closing costs, interest rates, and terms of loans, this simple tool in Excel can give you instant, accurate information to help you make the best decisions. If you don't have a computer with Excel already loaded, chances are your library or a friend does. There are also a lot of payment calculators on personal finance websites, but none are as convenient or fast as this one. Also, by moving from cell to cell in your spreadsheet, you can save your calculations and make notes next to each as you compare various loan packages.

For those souls not feeling technically savvy at this point, fear not. In the back of the book we've put the amortization factors and a neat explanation of how to calculate a payment.

Duration of the Loan: Loan Term

Now let's look at how the term impacts the payment distribution. The term, or duration of the loan, is the amount of time you will be in debt to the lender. The term you select will impact your payment and total interest paid on the loan. If you want to keep your money invested outside of your home, you would pick a longer term. If you want to own your home quickly and have your money invested in your home, you would pick a shorter term.

Most borrowers back into the payment they want, based upon their monthly income and comfort level. Today, 30-year loans are common. That's not to say that you cannot find a 15-year loan or a 40-year loan. Let's consider what might happen if, rather than borrowing for 30 years, we look toward a shorter loan repayment.

Remember, as you repay a loan, you're increasing your house's "savings account." So it stands to reason that the faster you can pay back a loan, the more money you have saved in your home. The figures in the following table are all assuming the same 6 percent interest rate and loan amount of $145,400.00 for 36 months.

If you had chosen a 25-year term rather than a 30-year, your payment would be $65.06 more a month. But your remaining loan balance now is $137,146.92. Another way to look at this is that you now own $2,559.18 more of this home because of the shorter term.

Loan Term	Monthly P&I Payment	Total of 36 Payments	Principal Amount Paid	Interest Amount Paid	Remaining Loan Balance
15 year	1,226.97	44,170.92	19,666.88	24,504.04	125,733.12
20 year	1,041.69	37,500.84	12,378.68	25,122.16	133,021.32
25 year	936.81	33,725.16	8,253.08	25,472.08	137,146.92
30 year	871.75	31,383.00	5,693.90	25,689.10	139,706.10
40 year	800.01	28,800.36	2,871.81	25,928.47	142,528.11

Diversity is key in any savings plan, and, at the end of the day, you certainly would not want all of your net worth to be in your home. In case of an emergency, or as you near retirement, it's very important to have had the opportunity to take advantage of other investments and their returns. To own your home is an American dream. But understanding how that dream equates to a financial decision enables you to leverage yourself in a manner that, in the future, you have some type of return on your money.

Pre-Payment Options

So let's say you don't want to tie yourself into a higher monthly payment, but like the idea of watching the balance you owe go down more than what a typical payment reduces it. As part of your lender interview worksheet (from Chapter 2), you'll notice the question "Do you have a pre-payment penalty on this loan?" No matter what type of loan you're looking at, I always recommend that you discuss the option of pre-payment. To pre-pay means that the lender has given you permission to pay the minimum payment each month plus an additional amount of your choosing, which would be applied toward the principal.

There are, however, lenders that will fine you or charge you a pre-payment penalty if you try to pay extra each month or pay off the outstanding balance early. Remember, the lender makes money each month that you have that loan, and, in some cases, they'd like to discourage you from paying it off any sooner than they would break even from a profit standpoint (i.e., in the event they made the loan at a deeply discounted initial interest rate). So always ask the question "Is there any penalty for pre-payment, either monthly or if I decide to pay off the entire balance with a refinance?" and confirm their answer, even before signing the final documents. The *Truth in Lending Disclosure Statement* discussed in Chapter 5 has a box the lender needs to mark if the penalty exists.

You will want to consider the overall impact of pre-paying your loan when it comes to your long-term goals. Your home is only one of several assets you will collect in your lifetime and it is usually one of the least liquid, which means you cannot get the cash as easily. As you plan for your future, it's important to not have all of your eggs in one basket. In times of high return on your dollar, you may want to take some of your extra money and invest it for a more favorable return, say, in mutual funds or stocks. A financial planner can help you to sort out what might be the best for you based upon your long-term objectives.

Now that you understand the mechanics of a mortgage loan, it is time to explore the different loan programs available. Lenders may or may not offer each of the programs we review, so once you zero in on a loan solution that feels right, you may be guided toward specific lenders.

Loan Categories: FHA, VA, Conventional

Before you begin your search for loan solutions, it's important to familiarize yourself with the categories of loans available.

The three basic loan categories for conforming loans are FHA (Federal Housing Administration), VA (Veteran's Administration), and conventional mortgage loans. The next segment of this chapter will educate you on each type. We will compare the loans for you, to help you define which may be the most likely to suit your needs. But not each loan category has the same specifications; so at the same time we're offering comparison, understand that all three require different documentation and different requirements.

For example, if you are eligible for a VA home loan, you'll find details that will aid you in getting yourself prepared to finance. And based upon general guidelines, you will see why the lender may recommend FHA financing before conventional for your purchase. There's a lot of great information in this section about both FHA and VA mortgages. Because they are regulated by government agencies, there are more requirements and regulations than for conventional mortgages. But don't let the requirements dissuade you from applying for the government loans; there are a lot of buyers that couldn't buy without these tremendous loan solutions.

FHA Mortgage Loans

The Federal Housing Administration (FHA) helps to provide government-insured loans by encouraging banks to lend to buyers with lower down payment requirements. The program was started in 1934 to create jobs by rebuilding and updating homes to stimulate the economy after World War II. FHA itself is not a lender. Instead, they "assure" the lender that they will receive their repayment, even if the borrower defaults, or doesn't pay on the loan. How can they do this, you might ask? Because FHA offers the lender an insurance, *which the borrower pays for*, known as MIP (mortgage insurance premium).

Mortgage Insurance Premiums (MIP)

FHA mortgage insurance premiums have been modified over the years. When the program began, premiums were paid on a monthly basis, calculated at .50 times the loan amount divided by 12 months. Today, that calculation is still valid, however, the program realized a severe shortage in funds in the late 1980s, and an additional premium was added to increase revenues in the early 1990s. Using our same $100,000 mortgage example, here is how you can expect the insurance to be calculated today:

Mortgage amount ($100,000.00) × MIP financed (2.25%) = Total loan amount ($102,250.00)

Total loan amount ($102,250.00) × MIP monthly (.50) = $511.25 MIP yearly

$511.25 MIP yearly ÷ 12 months = $42.60 per month

The MIP insurance can be compared to the Private Mortgage Insurance for conventional loans, and is discussed in the "Private Mortgage Insurance (PMI)" section. FHA's insurance is mandatory regardless of the borrower's future equity position in the property. The term of FHA's insurance is seven years, at the end of which time the full amount of the insurance premium has been earned.

FHA loans were once thought of as a first-time buyer loan, and although they've been used repeatedly as such, they are not only for that purpose. Because the required cash investment is 3 percent of the sales price, FHA can be a nice loan solution for someone who doesn't have a lot of money or is not interested in putting as much into the purchase. And if the money for the down payment is from a gift, perhaps from a parent or relative, FHA has no requirement for you having your own savings.

There is also the opportunity to finance a portion of the closing costs as part of the loan. Overall, FHA can allow for a lower cash outlay.

FHA Government Regulations

FHA highly regulates their lending practices; they have set maximum mortgage limits based upon median housing expenses within each region of the country. Therefore, when considering FHA financing, you should investigate the maximum allowable loan limits for your area. Check in at FHA's website at www.hud.gov in the information for homebuyer's section for a list that will provide the maximum mortgage limit for your area.

Bet You Didn't Know _____

The Department of Housing and Urban
Development in 1965 was made a cabinet-
level agency since HUD has positively
influenced the quality and availability of
housing for minorities, low- to moderate-
income households, and the elderly. The
Department of Housing and Urban Development has a tremendous website at
www.hud.gov.

The government statute that put FHA into place set
up different loan types that could be given. 203(b)
loans are the most common loans for one to four
family owner-occupied purchases. Other sections
that are commonly used today include the 703(b),
which was recently added to allow for loans to be
done on condominiums, and the 203(k) loans,
which are renovation loan programs. Not as often
seen but also available are the 203(i), which is the
program designated for financing manufactured
housing, and a 221(d) 2 loan that allows for a
modified down payment structure for low- to
moderate-income households.

The most popular financing solutions for FHA are
fixed financing and a 1 year adjustable rate mortgage. There is a complete explanation of financing
programs in Chapter 7.

VA Loans

The VA (Veterans Administration) was established as part of the Veterans Bill of Rights in 1944. Eligible veterans were given the opportunity to borrow 100 percent of the sales price of a home.

A VA loan is available to enlisted service personnel with continuous service for 181 days, a veteran with an honorable discharge, and any surviving spouse of an enlisted soldier killed in the line of duty. Reservists with 6-plus years of service or those enlisted who have seen active duty for 90-plus days during war time have been added to the list, expanding the benefit of the VA loan to tens of thousands.

Era	Dates	Time Required
WWII	9/16/40 to 7/25/47	90 days
Post WWII	7/26/47 to 6/26/50	181 days
Korean	6/27/50 to 1/21/55	90 days
Post Korean	2/01/55 to 8/04/64	181 days
Vietnam*	8/05/64 to 5/07/75	90 days
Post Vietnam	5/08/75 to 9/07/80	enlisted 181 days
	5/08/75 to 10/16/81	officers 181 days
	9/08/80 to 08/01/90	enlisted 2 years**
	10/17/81 to 08/01/90	officers 2 years**
Persian Gulf	8/02/90 to present	2 years

*The Vietnam Era began on 2/28/61 for those who served in the Republic of Vietnam.
**The veteran must have served 2 years or the full period of their orders, at least 90 days during wartime and 181 during peacetime.

The specific branch of the armed forces that the individual has been enlisted in issues a statement of service for enlisted personnel, or a DD-214, which is discharge orders. The DD-214 lists out the timeline that the veteran has been in service. The veteran sends this information on to the VA along with Form 1880, *Request for Certificate of Eligibility*. The certificate is needed because it lets the lender providing the financing know what amount of guarantee is available on the transaction. You can find and print this form at www.vba.va.gov/pubx/forms/26-1800.pdf.

VA Funding Fee

And rather than a monthly premium amount such as is required on FHA or conventional loans (which are covered next in this chapter), the VA charges a VA Funding Fee. The amount of this fee depends upon whether you're enlisted personnel or a reservist, and whether you've previously used your benefit or not. A benefit can be used more than once only if:

1. The original VA loan was paid in full.

2. The original VA loan was assumed by a veteran, who then substituted his or her entitlement for yours. Assumable loans are discussed in detail in Chapter 7.

The VA benefit was created to assist returning veterans buy homes and was not intended to allow a real estate investor create a rental portfolio from loans requiring little to no money down. There are other loan solutions available for that.

VA Funding Fee Tables

Purchase and Construction Loans

Type of Veteran	Down Payment	Percent of First Time Use	Percent for Subsequent Use
Regular	None	2.00	3.00*
Military	5% to 10%	1.50	1.50
	+10%	1.25	1.25
Reserve/	None	2.75	3.00*
Nat'l	5% to 10%	2.25	2.25
Guard	+10%	2.00	2.00

Cash Out Refinance

Regular Military		2.00	3.00*
Reserve/ Nat'l Guard		2.75	3.00*

Other Loans

Interest Rate Reduction Refinance Loan	.50	.50
Manufactured Home	1.00	1.00
Loan Assumptions	.50	.50

An exception is if veteran's prior use of entitlement was for a manufactured home loan.

VA Qualifying Guidelines

Qualifying guidelines will include ratio calculations as well as a residual income threshold. The residual income, or money left after paying the bills, is calculated by adding the total monthly housing expenses (see Chapter 1), utilities, maintenance expenses, and all long-term debt together. This number is then subtracted from the veteran's net income (after-tax take-home income). There is a minimum amount that must be left over in order to proceed. And this amount depends upon what region of the country you are buying in, the sales price, and the number of household members.

Table of Residual Income by Region (Loans $79,999 and Below)

Family Size	Northeast	Midwest	South	West
1	$390	$382	$382	$425
2	$654	$641	$641	$713
3	$788	$772	$772	$859
4	$888	$868	$868	$967
5*	$921	$902	$902	$1,104

Over 5 add $75 for each additional member up to 7.

Table of Residual Income by Region (Loans $80,000 and Over)

Family Size	Northeast	Midwest	South	West
1	$450	$441	$441	$491
2	$755	$738	$738	$823
3	$909	$889	$889	$990
4	$1,025	$1,003	$1,003	$1,117
5*	$1,062	$1,039	$1,039	$1,158

Over 5 add $80 for each additional member up to 7.

Region geographic areas for proceeding charts:

- **Northeast:** Connecticut, Maine, Massachusetts, New Hampshire, New Jersey, New York, Pennsylvania, Rhode Island, Vermont

- **Midwest:** Illinois, Indiana, Iowa, Kansas, Michigan, Minnesota, Missouri, Nebraska, North Dakota, Ohio, South Dakota, Wisconsin

- **South:** Alabama, Arkansas, Delaware, District of Columbia, Florida, Georgia, Kentucky, Louisiana, Maryland, Mississippi, North Carolina, Oklahoma, Puerto Rico, South Carolina, Tennessee, Texas, Virginia, West Virginia

- **West:** Alaska, Arizona, California, Colorado, Hawaii, Idaho, Montana, Nevada, New Mexico, Oregon, Utah, Washington, Wyoming

Unlike FHA (MIP) and conventional financing (PMI), there is no insurance premium. Rather, the Veteran's Administration offers a guarantee to the lender that they will reimburse their loss up to a certain percentage of the overall loan amount should the veteran default. The loan benefit is only good on a single-family or multi-unit dwelling that is owner-occupied.

The distinctive benefit to the VA is that no money is needed for the down payment. The VA is very protective of its program, and has gone so far as to state what fees can and cannot be paid for by the borrower. When considering a VA mortgage loan, you will be asking the seller to pay a portion of your loan expenses. Depending upon your purchase contract negotiation, veterans can often find themselves with no money needed at the loan closing. They can ask the seller through negotiations to pay 100 percent of their fees.

The maximum loan amount for a VA loan depends upon the conduit the lender uses for the mortgage in the secondary market and what the loan is being used for. If GNMA is used today for a purchase, the maximum is $203,000, which would also include the VA funding fee. The VA website for additional details and particulars of financing is www.homeloans. va.gov. Most VA loans are financed with a fixed term, usually 15 or 30 years.

Conventional Mortgages

Conventional mortgage loans are traditional financing solutions, dating back to the late 1800s. Today, conventional financing refers to loans without government-sponsored guarantees made by commercial lenders. For many decades, loans were only done when the borrower could provide significant down payments. As FHA and VA financing became more prevalent, banks and thrifts needed to become more competitive in their lending practices if they hoped to compete with that business. With the help of the private mortgage insurance industry, lenders became confident that they would be able to hedge their risks on lower down payment loans.

Private Mortgage Insurance (PMI)

And conventional loans have come a long way. Loans once needing a minimum 50 percent down payment today can be done with as little as 3 percent down. The Private Mortgage Insurance (PMI) industry developed as more borrowers wanted conventional loans, but didn't have large down payments. Mimicking FHA's insurance, these companies created a premium plan that would afford them the revenue needed to insure the loss should the borrower become unable to meet his or her obligation. And as with FHA loans, if a loan is not paid back to the lender, this insurance will guarantee the lender receives a percentage of the default amount back.

The private mortgage insurance premium is calculated, as is FHA's insurance, as a percentage of the loan amount. For example, for a loan with a down payment of 5 percent, the insurance will be higher than for a loan with a 10 or 15 percent down payment. And the insurance may be different for each type of loan product, such as adjustable rate or balloon (see Chapter 7 for details on these loan programs). Unlike FHA/MIP, the premium can either be financed or paid monthly.

Historically, PMI has been required on loans with less than a 20 percent down payment. It is paid begrudgingly because there is no perceived benefit to the borrower. So there have been some innovative loan solutions introduced into the marketplace the last few years that bypass the need. Chapter 8 has a section devoted to avoiding the PMI, should you be inclined to do so.

Unlike FHA/MIP, the premium will either be 100 percent financed or paid monthly. And there are ways to avoid mortgage insurance completely on a conventional loan, whereas FHA's insurance is mandatory and cannot be removed until 7 years have elapsed.

If you do take a loan with mortgage insurance, it is possible that after a couple of years you may consider removing the insurance. You can rewrite the loan (refinances are covered in Chapter 10) for a new loan if the lender determines with a new appraisal that you now have 20 percent in equity. You may also petition the lender for the mortgage insurance to be removed on the existing loan. There are specific guidelines in place to remove insurance that protect both the lender and the borrower. Chapter 5 offers insight on how to eliminate PMI.

The lender will consider whether you have been occupying the home at least 12 to 24 months, you have made payments as agreed, you still reside in the property, and there is proof that the home value is high enough in relationship to the loan to warrant removal of the insurance. The lender will request an appraisal or the equivalent to substantiate value. If it is determined that there is now 20 percent equity in the home, the lender may remove the insurance. It must be stressed here that it is the lender's discretion that will determine if the insurance will be removed.

Other Conventional Triggers

As you compare lending solutions there are a few other triggers that may help to determine your financing path. For example, most of the conventional loan programs still require that you save some of your down payment on your own, rather than borrow the funds from another source. FHA lets you obtain 100 percent gift if needed, and VA has no cash needed requirements. Down payment requirements are discussed in detail in Chapter 8, and the amount and source of funds often determine the best loan solutions.

Bet You Didn't Know

The term "conventional" refers to loans that follow the same pattern, having some conformity. You will hear these loans also referred to as "conforming" loans. Therefore, for loans that perhaps have atypical circumstances, one might find it necessary to look at alternative solutions or sub-prime loans.

The amount of the loan may also determine the loan solution. Conventional loan limits are based upon national median mortgage sales and are adjusted normally toward the end of the year. FHA and VA loan limits have not kept pace with the conventional loans. Currently, as of 2003, the maximum conforming loan limits are as follows:

Single family	$322,700
Two Units	$413,100
Three Units	$499,300
Four Units	$620,500

These limits are set nationally, with exceptions being Alaska, Hawaii, Guam, and the U.S. Virgin Islands. Their limits are 1.5 times the set amount.

The next logical question is "But what about loans that are higher than these limits?" Any loans beyond these limits are referred to as jumbo loans, also known as nonconforming loans. This is another time you may hear the term "nonconforming" used, but to a certain degree it makes sense. The loan limit does not meet the "norm," that being $322,700 or lower.

Jumbo loans are available for any loan above the conforming limit, but there can be a few differences. The market is somewhat limited for these products, meaning not as many lenders offer financing solutions for these clients. Jumbo loan rates are typically higher than for conforming loan amounts due to the greater risk taken by the lender in making this type of loan.

The loan guidelines may also change, although they are not unlike the conforming loans. The lender may require greater down payments on some loans; whereas 5 percent is standard on conventional financing, some loan programs may require 10 percent in this category. Income, asset, and credit expectations, however, should not differ.

Bet You Didn't Know

After World War II, plots of land were given to returning veterans for $1.00 per acre. The government felt as though this would not only offer veterans a place to build their homes, but it would also bolster the economy with remodeling. More than a million construction workers were out of work at the time. Many homes were built, and the economy slowly came back around, providing housing along the way.

Conventional financing also differs in another way. There are more choices of loan programs to choose from. Lenders are able to more readily develop loan solutions based upon changing economic climates and market segments. Therefore, conventional financing offers a broader range of programs than FHA and VA. As part of your selection you will find there are balloon loans, as well as a variety of adjustable-rate mortgage loan programs available. Each, as you will read in Chapter 7, can have its own set of parameters to follow, which can also make the process more confusing, but you also have more ways to tailor a loan for your specific needs.

The Least You Need to Know

- FHA mortgages offer an opportunity to purchase with lower cash requirements because often the closing costs can be financed.

- VA mortgages are appealing to eligible borrowers because they allow for 100 percent financing.

- When a mortgage is amortized, initially more of each payment is made towards paying back the principal balance of the loan.

- Any pre-payment of principal (also referred to as a curtailment) will reduce the amount of interest paid back to the lender.

Deciding on the Loan Program

In This Chapter

- Fixed- and adjustable-rate mortgages
- Balloon and graduated-payment mortgages
- Interest-only and assumable loans
- Making the loan decision that's best for you

There are as many different varieties of loans as there are flavors of ice cream. And because you are making some long-range plans when buying this home, it only makes sense that you would want to explore several options.

This list will offer general information meant to guide you in understanding the different products, but you must remember that each individual lending institution may offer its own twist.

For example, if you are interested in FHA financing because of the lower cash needed, not every loan listed here is eligible for FHA financing. Each category has its own loan programs.

Fixed-Rate Loans

"Fixed rate" means that the interest rate does not change, and therefore the principal and interest payment you make stays the same for the term of the mortgage note. The term refers to the number of years the loan will be repaid in. The note is the official document or IOU that says that you owe the money you are borrowing. The amount you pay to the lender will only vary as the payments for taxes and insurance change. Remember from Chapter 1 that taxes and insurance may be periodically adjusted as those expenses change for the respective party.

There are several different terms of fixed-rate loans. Most common is the 30-year fixed, but most lenders will accept terms of 25, 20, 15, and 10 years. FHA, VA, and conventional loan financing all have fixed-rate loans to choose from.

People who choose the fixed-rate loan option like the predictability of the payment and never need to worry about a rising interest-rate market. But as interest rates come down, they must consider a refinancing of their loan to take advantage of a lower rate and/or a lower payment.

As you pre-pay a fixed-rate mortgage, your payment never changes, as we said, but the term, or amortization period, will decrease. You can always check your progress by charting your pre-payment on an amortization schedule.

Adjustable-Rate Mortgage (ARM)

An adjustable-rate mortgage, also known as a variable-rate loan, means that the interest rate is going to move, and if the rate is moving, so is the monthly payment. ARM loans became popular in the late 1980s as fixed interest rates hit a whopping 18 percent. As you can imagine, the housing market was almost paralyzed. People wanted to buy homes, but very few could afford to. So the attractive lower initial rates on adjustable rate mortgages offered by lenders became very attractive, and actually helped the economy to rebound. Housing plays a pivotal role in how well our economy does.

Because of their shorter terms, a lender can afford to offer these loan products at lower rates, also known as "teaser" rates. These below-the-market interest rates usually last for a predetermined time, some as short as three months in duration. They are meant to attract the buyers who might otherwise put off their purchase until they perceive themselves to be better qualified to buy.

But we cannot forget that the rate is meant to be low for only so long. It is going to go up. And it's the higher rate that keeps a lot of buyers away from this type of loan. In order to make a decision for yourself, it's important to learn how the ARM loans move around.

The Adjustments

There are several different terms available when exploring ARM loans. The adjustment schedule refers to how often you can expect the interest rate to change. Adjustable-rate loans come in all configurations, so I suggest that you ask lots of questions to educate yourself. And they will definitely vary from lender to lender, so don't expect there to be a steadfast rule. But it's not uncommon to see ARMs offered in one-, three-, five-, seven-, or ten-year terms. Each "term" refers to a period of time that the loan interest will be set or fixed at a particular rate. For example, a three- or five-year ARM will have a rate fixed for three or five years respectively.

What happens at the end of the initial fixed period you ask? That depends upon the loan you are referring to. For example, a 3/3 ARM means that the rate is fixed for three years, and at the end of three years, the rate will be reset for another three years. A 3/1 ARM means that the rate is fixed for three years, but at the end of the three years, the rate will adjust each year.

The good news about these adjustments is that you know about them in advance, so you can prepare yourself for the movement. There are parameters that are also preset, known as adjustment "caps" and "life of loan "caps that restrict the amount that an interest rate can rise or fall. For example, FHA has available a one-year ARM loan product. This means that each year the interest rate is going to change. The caps that have been set by FHA are a maximum 1 percent annual payment cap and a 5 percent lifetime cap. This means that each year your payment may move by as much as 1 percent in interest rate over what it currently is, but no more than, plus-5 percent total.

So as a consumer, let's say your starting rate is 5 percent; next year you know your rate will be no higher than 6 percent, and the following year 7 percent. And over the entire life of the loan, your rate will be no higher than 10 percent, which is 5 percent over the starting rate. So you rarely can be caught offguard when it comes to how the rate will change. But these caps are specific to each loan, so it's a must to ask about them each time you explore a new lender's products. And although FHA's one-year ARM is 1/5 caps, most conventional loan products are 2 percent maximum annual and 5 to 6 percent maximum over the life of the loan (this is based on the index, see the section that follows).

It's also a great time to point out that you have some control over how the payment will move. We talked about how a pre-payment on the fixed-rate loan will not affect the amount of the payment but you will end up paying fewer months, accelerating your amortization. On an ARM loan, as you pre-pay, your loan balance is reduced in the same way it is on the fixed rate. But each time your interest rate is adjusted, the new payment is calculated on the outstanding principal balance at that time for the remaining term. You still have the same amortization, or number of years, to pay the loan, but your new payment will be related to how much you owe at the time.

For example, Jody is borrowing $120,000 for a condominium, knowing that she wants to move on to a home within 5 to 10 years. She has a choice of a 6.0 percent fixed rate, with a payment of $720/month, or a 4.5 percent ARM rate with a payment of

$609/month. If she chooses the ARM loan but makes a payment equal to the fixed contract, then she will have $111/month extra applied toward principal, or $1,332 more in equity in her condo at the end of the first year. This is money that will always be hers to add to her net worth. Even if her ARM rate increases by 1 percent the next year to 5.5 percent, her new loan payment will be calculated based upon the new loan amount of $117,150. Because she has prepaid her mortgage, Jody will never pay interest on the $1,332. Her new payment is now $665, but it is still less than the amount she would have paid on the 30-year loan, and she has created a higher net worth for herself by saving on interest expense.

So if you know you'd like to keep your payment within a range, try to pre-pay the loan balance. As the principal comes down, even if the interest rate rises, you won't feel the full effect of the increase. You can use the rate charts in the back of this book to play around with different scenarios to find the one that may work for you. We'll review the payment calculations in the next chapter.

In order to determine how much to pre-pay, and how much you can expect a payment to change, you must first understand what makes an ARM interest rate fluctuate.

The Index

Adjustable-rate loans will typically adjust based upon the movement of some money source. This money-related item is also referred to as the *index*.

As the value of this index goes up and down, so does the ARM loan rate. The following is a list of the most widely seen indexes used to set payments:

Mortgage Speak

The **index** is the money source that drives the movement of an adjustable loan product, such as the one-three-five-year Treasury securities.

- **Treasury Bills,** also known as **T-Bills,** are used as an index to base the common indicator for the movement of adjustable-rate loans in the Midwest and northern regions of the country.

- The **11th District Cost of Funds Index** was developed to measure the rates paid to depositors on the West Coast. This index has been popular for loans in the western United States.

- The London Interbank Offered Rate, also known as **LIBOR,** has become a popular indicator because it is a lagging index. In other words, it is not immediately impacted by market changes.

- The **Prime Lending Rate** is the rate that banks charge their best clients. The prime rate usually changes as the Federal Reserve amends its monetary policy.

The index may change hourly, daily, or weekly. But the interest rate will only change as often as its pre-set adjustments will allow for. If you have a volatile index, one that moves freely, then you will see your payment move more frequently.

The Margin

In all good equations, there is a variable quotient and a fixed factor that work the calculation. The fixed piece here is known as the *margin*. It has also been said that this is the lender's cut or profit on the loan. When shopping for an ARM loan, be sure to ask the margin, because it has already been decided and will stay fixed throughout the duration of the loan. The margin can be whatever the lender feels is appropriate, but it is usually 2 to 3 percent over the amount of the current index.

Mortgage Speak

The **margin** is the amount a lender adds to the index on an adjustable-rate mortgage to establish the interest rate; it is sometimes noted as the profit margin to the lender.

To illustrate, say that the index or money source is the U.S. Treasury Securities Index, and today it's at 3.05. A typical margin is 2.75 percent. Today's fixed-interest rate is probably 6 percent +/–. But the lender may be offering a bargain rate of 5.00 percent on a five-year ARM. And let's say that at the thirty-fifth month, the index has moved to 4.25. To determine what the new rate is, you add the current index to the always-constant margin, and round up to the nearest ⅛. The new rate after the third year would be 7 percent (2.75 + 4.25).

Caps

And remember, when you adjust, there are already maximum adjustments allowed because of the rate and life of loan *caps*. So what happens if the index-plus-margin total sum indicates that your payment should increase by 3 percent? That's the beauty of the caps—no matter what the index and margin add up to, the rate cannot exceed the caps. And on the other hand, if the index and margin do not total the full adjustment amount, it's possible to only move 1 or 1.375 percent. The caps are not in place to set the rate, only to keep the rate moving within a pre-determined acceptable range.

Mortgage Speak

A **cap** on interest is the maximum rate increase allowable per the loan as a protection to the borrower. A cap on payment is the maximum payment increase allowable per the loan as a protection to the borrower.

Negative Amortization

When shopping for a loan, ask if the rate and the payment change at the same time. If the rate and payment move at the same time, then that means you are making a payment that will allow the loan to be paid off within its term.

If, however, the rate and payment don't change at the same time, it's then possible for the interest rate to go up, but for the payment to stay the same. If that happens, the payment being made is probably not enough to cover the required principal and interest.

Unless you decide to pay extra each month to make up the difference, the lender now needs to add on to the outstanding balance. This is called *negative amortization*. In other words, you're not paying off the principle balance; you're incurring more balance. And that's not a good thing!

Mortgage Speak

Negative amortization is when the interest rate and payment do not change at the same time, causing the payment to be lower than what should be made to adequately cover the principal and interest portions of the scheduled payment, causing more interest to accrue.

Balloon Loans

Balloon loans usually are set with five-, seven-, or ten-year payoffs. Structured like a fixed-rate mortgage, payments are applied to an outstanding balance each month. At the end of the specified term, the note calls for the loan to be due and payable.

For example, on a seven-year balloon, at the end of the eighty-fourth month, the lender expects their remaining loan be paid off in its entirety. So why would a borrower put him- or herself into such a program? These loans are appealing to homebuyers because they are usually offered by the lender at 0.375 to 0.50 percent lower than a 30-year loan. And the astute homebuyer at this point has a plan and knows what this purchase means to him or her. The buyer is also aware that the average homeowner may only stay in his or her home for five to seven years. It's no coincidence this mortgage product has become very popular.

And if you decide you want to keep this loan ongoing? There are provisions in the note that say as long as you are willing to pay a small fee to the lender, you've made your payments as agreed, and you still live in the home, then they will consider extending the loan through the remaining term for a slight rate increase. Another option is to refinance the loan. Refinancing is discussed in Chapter 10.

Graduated Payment Loans (GPM)

Like adjustable-rate mortgage loans, the graduated-payment mortgage was designed to keep loan payments down initially, to encourage more home buying. In other words, the payment is not enough monthly to pay off the balance in the remaining years. But because the payment may not be quite enough to cover the amount needed to properly amortize the loan, additional interest would potentially accrue. And rather than paying down the mortgage loan, your outstanding principal balance would actually go up, causing negative amortization.

These loan solutions, due to their risk of increase in overall interest to be paid, have not been popular for many years. But never say never. Like bell-bottom jeans, everything comes back.

Interest-Only Loans

As the name indicates, rather than pay principal, the loan payment is all interest. This loan solution became popular in areas of the country where real estate appreciation (the increase in home equity based upon how other homes have been selling) is high. The loan is similar to an ARM as far as its set-up, but rather than amortizing as a home loan and applying a bit of the payment toward the principal amount borrowed, each monthly payment pays simple interest. If you never pay more than the minimum required at the end of the term, you still owe what you borrowed. You can make additional payments, but ask the lender about pre-pay penalties.

For example, you may see an opportunity to do an interest-only loan, five-year ARM, at Prime Rate + 1. If you borrow $150,000 and only pay each month an interest payment of $678 and want to sell the home in three years, you'd still owe $150,000. The $678 monthly for those 36 months is still considered an interest deduction to you, so it may not be a bad idea.

For a borrower, not paying money toward principal can be a double-edged sword. On the one hand, the monthly payment is lower because you're not putting money into your home's savings account by building equity. On the other hand, the payment is lower, and could be more affordable. And in real estate markets that have seen a hearty increase in values, is it necessary to add to the equity each month?

Assumable Loans

There are mortgage loans that include a provision that will allow the loan to be taken over, or the liability "assumed." The terms of the note can be carried over from one owner to another. For example, let's say that there is a seller who is offering their home for $147,000 and their loan is assumable. The rate was 6 percent when they bought the home 2 years ago and they owe $134,000 today.

If you were to take out a new mortgage loan today, the rates are at 7.25 percent. If you have the money for the down payment on this loan, the $13,000, you may be tempted to take the seller's loan vs. get a new one at the higher rate. When the loan is assumable, you not only take over the interest rate. It means that you will need to pay the seller the difference between what they owe and what they ask for their home in down payment.

Not all loans can be assumed; only those containing an "assumption clause" in their mortgage documents are assumable. Usually, fixed rate loans and their related products, such as a balloon loan, cannot be assumed. It's more likely you will find an ARM loan that is assumable.

The Lender's Role

The financing options are endless, and rather than take yourself down the wrong path, or not know enough to take a left rather than a right, educate yourself through the experts. This is why it's imperative that you find someone you like *and can understand* when choosing a lender. You've determined the monthly payment you're comfortable with. Based upon current market rates, you now know your maximum mortgage amount. Once you figure in the down payment, the lender can run scenarios on different loan solutions.

The questions I always ask are "How long can you envision yourself in this home?" or, at the very least, "How long can you see yourself in this mortgage?" If this is your first home, chances are higher that you'll probably not be there 30 years, and if you're not going to be there 30 years, do you need a 30-year loan? Sometimes the answer is yes, depending on your need for security. An ARM or balloon means that in a few years, if you wish to stay in your home, you'll need to consider another financing solution possibly. And we've said that no one yet has accurately read the future markets, so rates could be higher, or they may be lower. Some people cope with that idea well, while others couldn't sleep at night with that uncertainty. And again, you're the one with the checkbook, so you've got to determine where your comfort level lies.

You may never have all of the answers exactly right from the beginning, but taking time to plan what the loan means for you is crucial. It's different for everyone, because no two sets of circumstances are the same. Keep that in mind as you get bombarded with advice from friends, family, and colleagues who have gone through the home-loan process before you. You cannot make a bad decision if you've done your homework, and have chosen the loan based upon your situation, as you know it to be.

The Least You Need to Know

- Fixed rate means that the interest rate does not change, and therefore the principal and interest payment you make stays the same for the term of the mortgage note.

- When shopping for adjustable-rate mortgage (ARM) loans, ask about the index (the money source the loan is adjusted in accordance with) and the margin (the lender's number on top of the index), which will determine the maximum potential rate movement.

- Balloon mortgages are amortized like a fixed-rate loan, but the note is called due usually 5 or 7 years into the loan; rates are typically slightly lower than fixed rate because of their shorter duration.

- There are wonderful alternatives to fixed-rate financing, so explore all the options before thinking the fixed-rate loan is the only loan for you.

- Not all adjustable-rate loans have the same parameters. It's imperative that you discuss each loan program independently rather than assume all ARM loans contain similar terms.

Shopping for the Best Loan Package

In This Chapter

- How much to put down
- Shopping for a rate vs. shopping for a payment
- Discount points and buy-downs
- Creative solutions like no-PMI and combination loans

Money is a precious commodity, because it affords us the things we want and need. But it's also—in most cases—hard to come by. Mortgage brokers across the country are finding that most prospective borrowers have fine jobs and decent credit, but have little to no money saved. So it's only natural to want the best value for your dollars. But how do you know what the best use of that savings is? Well, that's the subject of this chapter.

Understanding the Down Payment

In the early 1800s, it was not uncommon to need more than 50 percent for a down payment before a bank would consider you as a potential customer. It has not always been easy to come up with that kind of savings quickly, and, as a result, the government got involved with financing that could benefit more potential home buyers. And today cash needed to purchase a home is considerably less than ever before. Let's learn the particulars.

A good place to start is with the amount of money you will need to put toward the purchase. The down payment is the difference between the price you pay for the home and the amount you need to borrow. For example, if you purchase a home for $161,600.00, a 10 percent down payment would be $16,160.00 ($161,600 × .10). The amount financed would then be $145,440.00 ($161,600 − $16,160).

There are minimum requirements we've touched on in this book, but here is a summary:

- On a conventional loan, the minimum down payment is in most cases 5 percent, although a few loan programs are available with 0 to 3 percent down. For almost all conventional mortgage loans, the borrower must be able to prove that he or she has a minimum of 5 percent savings in the purchase, and then any additional cash can be a gift from a parent or relative.

- On an FHA loan, your cash investment is a minimum of 3 percent, which is calculated on the sales price plus any allowable closing costs. And those monies can be your own savings, a gift, or a grant from a nonprofit group (more on this in the "No Down Payment?" section).

- On a VA loan, you are not required to have any down payment. If you do have cash to put into the purchase, the VA will reward you with a lower VA Funding Fee.

Understanding the Loan to Value

There are lending guidelines in place that speak to the *loan-to-value* relationship (*LTV*). We've been talking about the sales price up to this point, but it's really the value of the home that the lender is most concerned with. You can choose to pay whatever you like for a property, but the lender is only willing to lend you money based upon what they believe the home is worth. Another point to note here is that the lender bases everything they do off either the sales price or the appraised value, whichever is less.

Mortgage Speak _____

Loan to value (LTV) is a relationship expressed as a ratio between the property value of the home and the amount of the loan.

To help you understand the LTV, let's say a home is valued at $200,000, and you've paid $198,000. You may have a 20 percent down payment, so, even though the home is worth $200,000, your offer to purchase was $198,000; your down payment is $198,000 × .20 = $39,600, leaving you with a loan amount of $158,400. Your loan-to-value is 80 percent ($158,400 ÷ $198,000), even though the value came in at $200,000. Remember, the lender calculates based upon whichever is less, sales price or appraised value.

What if we had the same house that you've offered to pay $198,000 for, and the appraisal comes back to the lender at $195,000? You wanted a 20 percent down payment, but rather than calculate the 20 percent on the sales price, the lender will use the value in this case ($195,000 × .20 = $39,000). But now there's a dilemma because you have offered to pay $198,000, not $195,000. The lender will require you to come up with the additional $3000, for a total of $42,000. Because, again, they lend based upon the lesser of the two, sales versus appraisal.

It goes without saying here that you may not choose to pay more for a home than what the lender sets its value at. Or you may consider renegotiating with the seller if the price is higher than the value. Either way, you now know how to calculate the down payment. Here are some examples:

- If you have a 5 percent down payment, your LTV is 95 percent.
- If you have a 10 percent down payment, your LTV is 90 percent.

No Down Payment?

At one time, not so very long ago, unless you were a veteran, it was unheard of for a borrower to buy a home without a down payment. The lender, upon discovering there were not savings or gift monies available, usually structured a savings plan for the borrower until he or she had the sufficient amount of funds for a down payment.

Today, numerous programs are available that will assist borrowers without their own resources. For example, there are several nonprofit groups that will facilitate a grant with seller funding. Similar to the temporary buy-down concept in Chapter 7, the seller builds the cost of the down payment into the sales price, and offers to then "gift" the down payment through the nonprofit group for the mere cost of the administrative fees. A few examples are as follows:

- **Nehemiah:** www.nehemiahcorp.org
- **Neighborhood Gold:** www.neighborhoodgold.com
- **Ameridream:** www.ameridreamcharity.org

There are also local community initiatives that are always popping up to give buyer assistance. For example, the Community Reinvestment Act (CRA) requires some banks to give back to their communities, and many choose to do so in low- to moderate-income home loans with significantly reduced cash investments.

And still other lenders have chosen to experiment and offer no-down-payment loans to borrowers meeting high credit score requirements, for example, more than 700 (see Chapter 4 for more information about credit scores). The interest rates are usually higher, but it may make sense to you. Say you have the savings in stocks but it's not a good time to cash in your investments. You may be able to purchase a home and leave your stocks intact.

The Rate vs. Payment

First, I caution you against shopping solely for the lowest rate. In my experience, the borrower that focuses only on the interest rate is missing the bigger picture. Remember, it's not the interest rate you pay monthly, it's a house payment; the house payment is what needs to fit into your monthly budget. And although the rate is important in calculating the house payment, it is not the only factor. The savvy shopper understands the relationship between the rate and the cost of the rate.

Discount Points and the Permanent-Rate Buy-Down

Interest rates are available on a sliding scale. A rate is available that will not cost you extra money, and that rate also may be lowered if you're willing to pay some additional up-front fees. Said another way, the lower the interest rate, the higher the cost to obtain the rate. This practice is called "discounting" the interest rate. And, frankly, discounting the rate often makes no sense to the borrower.

To illustrate, let's say today's true market interest rate or "par rate" is 6.50 percent. The par rate means there are no added fees to get that particular rate. But you don't want to pay 6.50 percent; you'd like a lower rate, because lower is perceived as a better value (and maybe your neighbor got that rate a month ago). The lender might perhaps offer you a 6.25 percent rate, but ask you to pay an up-front fee, and, in return, provide you a lower rate for the term of your loan. The money paid up front is considered as paying *discount points*. In dollars, 1 discount point equals 1 percent of the loan amount; a rule of thumb is 1 point for each ⅛ to ¼ drop in the interest rate. This relationship will vary based on market conditions.

Mortgage Speak

A **discount point** is the cost associated with purchasing a lower interest rate than the prevailing market; it is considered pre-paid interest.

For example, on a $145,400 loan (30-year term) with a par rate of 6.5 percent, here are the calculations:

Payment at 6.5% is $918.93, no points

Your new rate: 6.25 = (6.5 − 0.25)

Payment at 6.25% is $895.67, for 1 point or $1,454.00

Your monthly payment savings—principal and interest: $23.26 = ($918.93 − $895.67)

Your recoup period: 62.51 months = ($1,454.00 ÷ $23.26)

Basically, you would need to stay in the home longer than 63 months (over 5 years) to recoup the cost of the discount points you paid.

Here is a snapshot view of how interest rates may vary on any given day. The concept to grasp here is that the lender truly does not care which rate combination you choose, because the net effect to them is the same. In other words, each of these rate scenarios will give the lender the same return. But you as a borrower may find that one will suit your purpose better than another.

The following table illustrates how rates may vary based upon how long you might need the interest rate to be guaranteed, or locked in from application to loan closing. As the number of days increase, so does the cost of the rate. Each point is calculated as a percentage of the loan amount. Usually, your purchase agreement will dictate the timeline in which the transaction must be performed, hence how long the rate lock must be in place.

Interest-Rate Comparison—30-Year Fixed Rate

Rate	15 Days	30 Days	60 Days
5.500	1.25 points	1.75 points	2.00 points
5.625	0.75 points	1.25 points	1.50 points
5.750	0.25 points	0.50 points	0.75 points
5.875	(0.25) points*	0.00 points	0.25 points
6.000	(0.75) points*	(0.25) points*	0.00 points
6.125	(1.50) points*	(1.00) points*	(0.75) points

Rates can be locked in for as many as 270 days, but typically the lender will charge an extended lock-in fee. Because there is no way to predict future market conditions, the up-front fee hedges their risk somewhat. Usually, there is no additional expense for transactions completed within 45 to 60 days.

* Denotes the point where the lender will actually pay you money for taking that rate. They will usually offer to pay closing-cost expenses. These monies cannot be used for the down payment.

For example, if you are negotiating with the seller on the sales price, you can try to include the cost of any discount points to buy down the rate. They probably will not negotiate as much on the price you pay, but you will build the cost of obtaining the rate into your loan.

This is the "pay me now or pay me later" approach to borrowing money. If you decide to pay extra today, your rate will be lower, but if you don't want to pay extra, your rate will be higher. And just because you're paying a lower interest rate doesn't mean that's a better loan. You've seen the impact of paying points, both monthly and as closing costs. You've also seen the monthly savings after paying to discount the rate.

A tool used by financial planners to evaluate the best way to go is a calculation called present value. Present value simply means to take into account the cost of doing business at today's price.

Discount points take time—in most cases, years—to recover. Ideally, when a borrower pays points up front to discount the interest rate, he or she should expect to be in the home long enough to recover the initial cash investment. The monthly savings experienced, then, is worthwhile. Otherwise, those dollars paid up front only benefit the lender. So just because the rate is lower, it doesn't mean that you're spending less money. That's why shopping for rate may not always give you the best results. Remember, it's the total cost of the loan that is important.

The Temporary Buy-Down

We've reviewed how you can pay to get a lower interest rate permanently on a mortgage loan. But a loan rate can also be brought down temporarily. This loan variation is known, as you might expect, as a temporary buy-down. With the help of a third party, for example, seller or builder, and lender, the borrower can take advantage of an interest rate that is below what the market may be offering.

The interest rate will increase over time, on a predetermined schedule, usually annually, until it is brought up to the rate the market would have been charging. The seller or builder may offer this option to help sell his or her home by creating more financing solutions for the buyer. Perceived lower interest rates lead to more traffic through a home. And there's no added overall expense to the seller because he or she will recover the expense of the temporary buy-down through the sales price of the home.

The following typical buy-down is a 2–1 with a 30-year term. The rate begins at 2 percent below the actual note rate the first year, at 1 percent below the rate the second year, and will increase to the note rate for the third to thirtieth years.

Buy-Down Terms

Rate		Term
4%	for	12 months (year 1)
5%	for	12 months (year 2)
6%	for	336 months (years 3 through 30)

A borrower might look at this financing solution for a couple of reasons. The initial rate is lower, and is often the rate you will be qualified at. For example, if our 2–1 buy-down is a note rate of 6 percent, the first year our payment will be calculated based upon an interest rate of 4 percent, the second year the rate will increase to 5 percent, and the third and remaining years the loan rate is the note rate, 6 percent. And as a borrower, you will probably qualify for more home at 4 percent (because your payment will be much lower), which may be important at the time.

Another reason you might consider this type of loan is if you have previously had a double income household, for example, but recently had a child and one party is staying at home for the next year or two. The mortgage payment will continue to rise each year, and cap out just as the second party returns to the work force (in time to help manage the increased mortgage payment).

I mentioned that the seller or builder usually offers the temporary interest rate buy-down to create foot traffic. It's like the ARM teaser rate: too low to pass up a look. From the seller's viewpoint, here's how it works:

We'll assume a sales price of $161,600, with a down payment of 5 percent. Temporary buy-downs are usually the most appealing to buyers with lower down payments because they'd love to have the money up front to lower their payments, but often do not. Our loan amount is $145,400. The builder has agreed to provide us with the 2–1 buy-down above: 4–5–6. Here's what happens:

- **Year 1:**
  P&I = $693.00 ÷ 56 @ 4%
  Note Rate = $872.40
  Difference $2,146.08 = $178.84 × 12

- **Year 2:**
  P&I = $780.80 @ 5%
  Note Rate = $872.40
  Difference $1,099.20 = $91.60 × 12

- **Years 3 through 30:**
  Note Rate = $872.40
  Total subsidy $3,345.28 = $2,146.08 + $1,099.20

The $3,345.28 is placed in a subsidy account with the lender. Each month in the first year, as the borrower pays $693.56, the lender will pull out $178.84 from the subsidy account and apply a total amount of $872.40. The same happens the second year. The borrower pays $780.80, the lender set aside is $91.60, with $872.40 being applied.

The builder or seller did not offer this financing for free. More likely, he or she has added the $3,345.28 (cost of financing the buy-down) to the sales price of the home, which then means that you have more than likely financed the cost of the buy-down over the loan term.

Is this a bad deal? Certainly not, if you consider the monthly savings, and assuming that you keep the home a number of years to allow the home's appreciation and your equity buildup to catch up with the $3,345.28 used as a financing concession.

PMI/MIP: Is There Another Way?

Mortgage insurance coverage has enabled lenders to loosen up on their restrictions over the years, allowing up to 95 percent financing on homes. By allowing purchases with as little as 5 percent down payment, the industry opened up home ownership to a tremendous number of new buyers. But many borrowers have voiced loud objections at the same time because of how expensive the insurance can sometimes be, and the fact that it's paid by the borrower but yet gives no direct benefit or protection to them.

Until recently it was impossible to get a loan with less than a 20 percent down payment without PMI. And FHA, as we said, always requires the insurance. Today, there are two other solutions to explore:

- Loans that require no PMI
- Loans that are a combination of first and second mortgages

Each of these types of loans will be covered in the sections that follow.

No-PMI Loans

There are loans known as no-PMI loans or loans with lender-paid mortgage insurance, LPMI loans. With as little as 5 percent down, the borrower can avoid the mortgage insurance by his or her willingness to accept a slightly higher interest rate. In order to pull off the higher rate, the mortgage industry keeps the interest rate just below what the PMI premium rates are. The interest rate is typically higher because the risk to the lender is greater without the insurance. (So you are paying for it anyway, but it is tax-deductible.)

But why would anyone take a higher interest rate over a lower rate? Because, if you put the two loans side by side, without the escrow monthly mortgage insurance, the overall housing expense is lower. But how could that be, you ask? Because the lending industry became very smart and realized that there probably wasn't as much risk to these higher LTV loans as what they had thought years ago. And they also realized that by self-insuring the loans, they were able to create another profitable series of loans, because they could charge more for the higher risk. And not only is your payment lower, but also, because you've increased your interest rate, your tax-deductible interest has also increased. And all for the lower payment.

First/Second Combination Loans (80/10/10) (80/15/5)

Most underwriting guidelines have always stated that it was all right for a borrower to take a second mortgage loan out against the savings (equity) in the home, as long as his or her lien was kept in first position. And it seems over the last five years, lots of homebuyers have taken full advantage of their equity by securing home-equity loans and lines of credit. We discuss these loans as they pertain to refinancing in Chapter 10, but they can also be helpful in avoiding the mortgage insurance when you are purchasing.

When you are taking out the loan, it is possible to do a combination first/second mortgage loan, also known as 80/10/10 and 80/15/5, to avoid the mortgage insurance. Here's how these loans work. Let's say you have a 10 percent down payment toward your home purchase. Consider a second loan for the additional 10 percent; total down payment is now 20 percent and you no longer need mortgage insurance. The same works with a 5 percent down payment and a second mortgage of 15 percent. The second mortgage can be repaid as an interest-only line of credit—or as an installment loan with a fixed payment. There is the additional interest tax deduction in most cases, also. Always check with your tax advisor on deductions.

The rate is usually lower on the *home-equity line of credit (HELOC)* than on the *home-equity loan*, because, as with first mortgages, the lender will usually charge a higher interest rate on a longer term. The following comparison will help you to understand your options. The HELOC is a variable rate, which means that it can go down and up as market conditions dictate.

Mortgage Speak

A **home-equity loan** is an installment loan that requires that the loan against the savings in the home be repaid in equal installments for a specified period of time, with definite beginning and ending dates. A **home-equity line of credit (HELOC)** is a revolving loan usually associated with the prime rate, which enables the homeowners to use their home's equity as collateral on a loan, with payments normally calculated with minimum interest only and no required principal reduction, usually available for up to 10 years.

Comparing Your Mortgage Insurance Options

So now, if you have less than 20 percent to put down on your home or you don't have 20 percent in equity in your home when you refinance, there are actually three different ways to finance:

- Traditional financing

  Example: Sales Price of $161,600 with 10 percent down = $16,200 down payment

  Total mortgage amount: $145,400 × .06 = $871.75 + $65.00 (per month PMI) = $936.75

- No-PMI financing

  Example: Sales Price of $161,600 with 10 percent down = $16,200 down payment

  Total mortgage amount: $145,400 × .06375 (higher rate) = $918.93 (no PMI needed)

- First/second combination loans

  Example: (80/10/10) Sales Price of $161,600 with 20 percent down = $32,320 down payment (10 percent cash and another 10 percent in a second mortgage)

  First Mortgage $129,250 × .06 = $775.60

  Second Mortgage $16,200 × .0625 (prime + rate) = $83.22

  Total Mortgage amount: First Mortgage ($775.60) + Second Mortgage ($83.22) = $858.85

It's Your Money

As mentioned earlier, the second mortgage can either be on a fixed payment or a HELOC with a flexible rate, interest only. For comparisons, this example is the lesser of the two payments, interest only. The home equity loan would be higher monthly, making the payment comparable to the no-PMI payment.

Each of these loan solutions accomplishes the purchase, but with different characteristics. The traditional method shows the payment plus PMI at $936.75, the no PMI shows the payment of $918.93, and the combination loan assumes $858.85.

Here are a few ideas to consider when making your comparison:

- How long will you be in the home? Mortgage insurance can eventually be removed. Do you really need to pay the higher interest rate or take a second mortgage? Check with your lender first regarding their criteria for removing mortgage insurance. Usually, PMI can be removed within 12 to 24 months. For FHA, when the loan balance is reduced to 78 percent of the original sales price or appraised value the insurance is no longer required. FHA's monthly insurance payment must be paid for a minimum of five years.

- Are you on a fixed budget? The predictability of the mortgage payment may be important. The lender-paid mortgage insurance may work well.

- Will you pre-pay this loan? If yes, you may like the first/second mortgage, because you could eliminate the second, and eventually only have the first mortgage without the monthly insurance cost.

- Is no mortgage insurance available? Not every lender offers it, and those that do may offer it only on specific products.

- Are there any additional costs associated with any of these options? Aside from the hike in interest rates on lender-paid mortgage insurance, there should be no additional extras.

Remember also that the average life expectancy of a mortgage is five to seven years, so it's also possible you would be in a position to refinance, no matter which loan you start with.

The Least You Need to Know

- The cash available to purchase, and the source of that down payment, many times will dictate the mortgage solution best suited for you.

- The lower rate may not always be the best deal for a borrower; reserve judgment until you take into consideration the cost of the rate and determine the payback years of that rate in relationship to the money it costs to obtain the rate.

- A temporary interest rate buy-down is typically offered by the seller or builder to create foot traffic through a property; the cost of the lower initial interest rate is most often built into the cost of the home.

- There are several different solutions available on a conventional loan with regards to mortgage insurance. It's prudent to review your options with the lender to determine which may be the best for your long-term objectives.

Chapter 9

Closing on the Loan

In This Chapter

- Escrow closings
- Round-table closings
- Your responsibility at the closing
- Understanding the HUD-1 settlement statement

The time has come to put you officially into debt. Up to now, there has not been any financial obligation between you and the lender. You could have at any time chosen to abandon the application, move to another company, or give up the idea entirely. You would have forfeited any money spent on your application fees and the time invested, but you hadn't committed yourself yet.

There will be a meeting where documents will be signed and the transactions will be final. This meeting is referred to as the "closing." Two things will happen at the closing. The seller will transfer the deed and title to the property over to you, and the mortgagor will transfer the money to the seller while placing a lien on your property.

The seller is also turning over the property to you, based upon your contractual agreement. You can expect the keys, garage door openers, as well as the manuals to the appliances.

But don't be alarmed if everything doesn't look perfect or go smoothly. Think about how many pieces need to come together at the same time and what needs to be reviewed, verified, and approved. The loan closing is notoriously known for rewrites and corrections. It's a time for patience but also for diligence, because everyone wants it right before it's all sealed and delivered.

Round-Table Closing vs. Escrow Closing

The closing is the culmination of the purchase or the lending process. Although there are documents for both the buyer and the seller to be signed, most of the paperwork is for the borrower. And depending upon which region of the country you're in and how your community is set up, you will either have a round-table closing or an escrow closing.

The round-table closing is the traditional method. Buyers and sellers have already decided as part of their purchase agreement the date of their settlement. And depending upon what may be customary in your marketplace, one of the parties will have been responsible for choosing the company that will facilitate the closing. Different parts of the country do it differently, but normally, the party that is responsible for paying the title insurance chooses the company.

Bet You Didn't Know

In the case of a refinance, the borrower chooses and will often return to the original settlement company because of discounts they may provide. Discounts include no survey, reduced closing fees, and credit on title insurance and the title search.

The traditional closing often took place in a bank office, with a representative of the bank facilitating the process. The buyers sat on one side of the table, the sellers on the other. If there was representation such as an attorney or a Realtor present, they took up seats next to their clients. There usually was an abstract of title that was reviewed. Often as thick as a small book, the abstract showed all of the ownership transfers and conveyances (transfer to title/ownership interest). The lender wanted to make certain that the buyer had free and clear ownership. The facilitator doled out the paperwork to be signed. At the end, everyone shook hands and exchanged keys and well wishes. The deal was done.

Today's process is much the same; however, rather than the transaction taking place at the bank's office, it is done at an independent third-party site, usually a title insurance company, escrow agent, or an attorney's office. In the early 1970s, banks chose to outsource the closing piece, both for efficiency and cost. This was also the time when mortgage money sources changed from primarily banks to the secondary market providers, Fannie Mae and Freddie Mac (see Chapter 7 for more information).

The description of closing could be portrayed in a Norman Rockwell print. But this closing is not without its own issues. If you're transacting with sellers, everyone needs to agree on a date and time. And there are lots of parties that need to make the same time commitment. Settlement companies have relaxed their scheduling to accommodate closing at two different hours on the same day if needed, but this is obviously duplication, thus not very cost-effective for them.

It can be more complicated when the seller is expecting his or her sales proceeds at closing and needs those funds to take to his or her loan closing on a new home. If there are delays or split times for signing, it may mean trips back and forth. But when it can be orchestrated, the process can be very pleasant.

An escrow closing is done differently. The earnest money is held by an independent title insurance representative, escrow company, or attorney. They become the money "pass-through" resource. All cash from buyer, seller, and lender pass through this agency. And rather than set a specific date and time for closing, "the escrow" is open for a few days to allow for all disbursements to arrive. The information is then reconciled, and, at the end of the window, disbursements are made and the keys delivered. Perhaps it's not as personal—the closing is, after all, a business transaction and is handled as such.

The Flow of Information

Regardless of whether you are in an area where your closing is round table or escrow, the movement of information and documentation is the same. Remember, the settlement agent is acting on behalf of the lender, as an intermediary for all parties. Think of this as the final act of a large production, where all parties come together for the grand finale. And usually there is a lot going on, and it's anything but smooth.

The lender provides the closing company with instructions on how the loan paperwork should read, what fees need to be charged, and how the borrowers will be taking title. The lender will also usually send along the necessary documents for signature. The Realtors and attorneys involved have provided copies of the purchase agreement or contract that spells out the terms and conditions of the transaction.

In the meantime, the closing agent is compiling information on services performed and fees charged for such things as the survey, the pest inspection, and county recorders office, to name a few. Anyone who participates in any facet of the home purchase/ home sale process that renders a service must be accounted for.

Then there is the research to make certain the property will be transferred correctly, with clear title. This means that someone will physically research county courthouse records to determine who may have placed a claim, lien, or encumbrance on the property in the recent past. Most of these services cannot be performed until after the mortgage is approved, which is usually only a couple of days before the loan is set to close.

So information comes to the settlement agent, and it is processed and reviewed and disbursed to the borrower, seller, and agents involved. And each of these participants must review and approve of those items they have brought to the table.

Usually, the settlement agent is providing the final dollar figure to the anxious borrower. And one of the most common complaints heard is how hard it is to get the final number. Is it any wonder, given the number of people and the task of accumulating all of the data needed?

A tip here is to get a worst-case scenario figure from the lender. They can usually provide you an accurate estimate and if your check is too much, the settlement agent will refund you the difference. Have the check made payable to yourself, so you can endorse it over once everything meets with your satisfaction.

It's always better to bring too much money rather than not enough. Most lenders cannot accept personal checks for any amount above $1,000.00.

The Documentation You'll Need to Have

If you don't pay cash for the home, then for a closing to take place, your lender will need to approve you for a loan and provide the settlement company with appropriate paperwork to be signed. And in their approval, they will have specified what you may need to complete the transaction with them. You should have been notified by letter of any outstanding conditions that need satisfied for them to grant your loan. Normal conditions are, for example, verification that you've received your funds from an investment plan for closing. It's prudent to have a talk with the lender before arriving at the closing, to refresh yourself on what is still needed. There is a lot of activity surrounding the closing, and it's easy to forget or misunderstand what's needed.

Bet You Didn't Know

Rather than being pressured to read the fine print at the loan closing, request the paperwork be available to read 24 to 48 hours prior to closing. Take it home the night before, read it, make notes on questions you may have. Then, at closing, the time is spent in summary, rather than bewilderment. Under federal law, the borrower has a right to receive the HUD-1 settlement statement 24 hours prior to closing.

The settlement company will also require a few things from you. In most states, a photo ID is required to prove that you are who you sign you are. You will also be asked to provide evidence of homeowner's insurance, usually a policy and a paid receipt to show you actually purchased it. The insurance policy is required regardless of whether you will be escrowing or not. The mortgage document specifies that you must have suitable insurance coverage at all times, and you must be able to provide proof at closing and upon request in the future.

The insurance provider will also ask you how the policy should be made out. The term they will most likely use is the mortgagee clause. Remember, you are in a partnership with the mortgage lender, and the policy will need to reflect the lender's name, address, and account number for reference. Should there be a need to file a claim, both the borrower and the mortgagee will be covered.

Bet You Didn't Know

Because of fraud, most lenders no longer allow you to close escrow with a personal check. Expect to be asked to provide a cashier's check or to arrange for funds to be "wired" or electronically transferred to the settlement agent. If you intend to wire funds, prepare in advance. It can sometimes take a lead time of a few days to coordinate the transfer.

Be prepared to have your funds available in the form of a cashier's check or some form of currency recognized as cash. The good-funds law in most states requires that the money you put on the table at closing be immediately tendered. You will learn of the amount needed to be brought to closing from your lender, your real estate agent, or the settlement company. And if you've received good information from your lender, it's close to what you've expected.

Bet You Didn't Know

On the refinance of an owner-occupied residence, the lender must allow you three days after closing to change your mind, know as a "rescission" period. This practice was established to allow the borrower a cooling off period, and to make certain that they had not signed their paperwork under duress. The three-day right to rescind is not required on investment properties and second homes.

The average loan closing takes about one hour, and that's not much time to read through the forms that will require your signature. You should schedule your closing in such a way that the documents can be made available to you a couple days in advance. That way, you have time to read, make notes, and look for any corrections before you get to the big event.

The HUD-1 Settlement Statement

It's hard to imagine how funds are dispersed if you've never been to a loan closing. There are expenses for the title company, the survey, the recorder's office, the home inspector, the termite company, the gas folks … and the list grows.

The HUD-1 Settlement Statement is a standard industry form that was designed to simplify the details. This document shows the expenses of the transaction. Both the borrower and seller, if applicable, are represented on the same form.

The HUD-1 identifies the parties involved, the property address, the loan number, lender name, and loan type. It is meant to be the reference tool for the closing and summarizes the disbursement of the money. The form is split, and all applicable expenses are listed in the respective columns, identified, and totaled. Any credits, such as application fees or earnest money, are also listed, so that at the bottom, when all has been added and subtracted, the funds needed to settle are disclosed. This is where you get the magic number for funds needed for closing.

By the time you get to the closing, you should have a clear understanding of what money you'll need to have available. Let's look at the HUD-1 and correlate this form to the Good Faith Estimate and Truth in Lending disclosures from the Uniform Residential Loan Application (see these in Chapter 3). We've learned that the forms should reflect approximately the same charges.

OMB NO. 2502-0265

U.S. DEPARTMENT OF HOUSING & URBAN DEVELOPMENT

SETTLEMENT STATEMENT

B. TYPE OF LOAN
1. ☐ FHA   2. ☐ FmHA   3. ☐ CONV. UNINS.   4. ☐ VA   5. ☒ CONV. INS.
6. FILE NUMBER   CARA   7. LOAN NUMBER   31112005
8. MORTGAGE INS CASE NUMBER

C. NOTE: This form is furnished to give you a statement of actual settlement costs. Amounts paid to and by the settlement agent are shown. Items marked "POC" were paid outside the closing; they are shown here for informational purposes and are not included in the totals.

1.0   3/98   (Cara.pfd/CARA/19)

D. NAME AND ADDRESS OF BORROWER	E. NAME AND ADDRESS OF SELLER	F. NAME AND ADDRESS OF LENDER
John Doe 123 Anywhere St. Columbus, OH 43220	Jane Doe 456 Nowhere Street Columbus, OH 43220	Megastar Financial 500 W. Wilson Bridge Road, #312 Worthington, OH 43085

G. PROPERTY LOCATION	H. SETTLEMENT AGENT 31-0730671	I. SETTLEMENT DATE
123 Anywhere Street Columbus, OH 43220 Franklin County, Ohio Parcel #123-456789	Northwest Title PLACE OF SETTLEMENT 5055 Dierker Road Columbus, Ohio 43220	May 30, 2003

The HUD-1 Settlement Statement—General Information.

J. SUMMARY OF BORROWER'S TRANSACTION		K. SUMMARY OF SELLER'S TRANSACTION	
100. GROSS AMOUNT DUE FROM BORROWER:		**400. GROSS AMOUNT DUE TO SELLER:**	
101. Contract Sales Price	161,600.00	401. Contract Sales Price	161,600.00
102. Personal Property		402. Personal Property	
103. Settlement Charges to Borrower (Line 1400)	2,948.32	403.	
104.		404.	
105.		405.	
Adjustments For Items Paid By Seller in advance		*Adjustments For Items Paid By Seller in advance*	
106. City/Town Taxes to		406. City/Town Taxes to	
107. County Taxes to		407. County Taxes to	
108. Assessments to		408. Assessments to	
109.		409.	
110.		410.	
111.		411.	
112.		412.	

Line Items 100 through 112 and 400 through 412.

120. GROSS AMOUNT DUE FROM BORROWER	164,548.32	420. GROSS AMOUNT DUE TO SELLER	161,600.00
200. AMOUNTS PAID BY OR IN BEHALF OF BORROWER:		500. REDUCTIONS IN AMOUNT DUE TO SELLER:	
201. Deposit or earnest money		501. Excess Deposit (See Instructions)	
202. Principal Amount of New Loan(s)	145,440.00	502. Settlement Charges to Seller (Line 1400)	11,544.10
203. Existing loan(s) taken subject to		503. Existing loan(s) taken subject to	
204.		504. Payoff of first Mortgage	
205.		505. Payoff of second Mortgage	
206.		506.	
207.		507.	
208.		508.	
209.		509.	
Adjustments For Items Unpaid By Seller		Adjustments For Items Unpaid By Seller	

Line Items 120 through 209 and 420 through 509 (and Adjustments).

210. City/Town Taxes		to		510. City/Town Taxes		to
211. County Taxes	07/01/02 to 05/30/03		2,187.00	511. County Taxes	07/01/02 to 05/30/03	2,187.00
212. Assessments	to			512. Assessments	to	
213.				513.		
214.				514.		
215.				515.		
216.				516.		
217.				517.		
218.				518.		
219.				519.		
220. *TOTAL PAID BY/FOR BORROWER*			147,627.00	520. *TOTAL REDUCT. AMT DUE SELLER*		13,731.10
300. **CASH AT SETTLEMENT FROM/TO BORROWER:**				600. **CASH AT SETTLEMENT TO/FROM SELLER:**		
301. Gross Amount Due From Borrower (Line 120)			164,548.32	601. Gross Amount Due To Seller (Line 420)		161,600.00
302. Less Amount Paid By/For Borrower (Line 220)			(147,627.00)	602. Less Reductions Due Seller (Line 520)		(13,731.10
303. *CASH (X FROM)(TO) BORROWER*			16,921.32	603. *CASH (X TO)(FROM) SELLER*		147,868.90

Line Items 210 through 303 and 510 through 603.

Page 2

L. SETTLEMENT CHARGES		PAID FROM BORROWER'S FUNDS AT SETTLEMENT	PAID FROM SELLER'S FUNDS AT SETTLEMENT
700. TOTAL COMMISSION Based on Price $ 161,600.00 @ 6.0000 % 9,696.00			
Division of Commission (line 700) as Follows:			
701. $ 4,848.00 to Ultimate Realty			
702. $ 4,848.00 to The Best Realty			
703. Commission Paid at Settlement			9,696.00
704.	to		
800. ITEMS PAYABLE IN CONNECTION WITH LOAN			
801. Loan Origination Fee % to			
802. Loan Discount % to			
803. Appraisal Fee to Megastar Financial		300.00	
804. Credit Report to Megastar Financial		50.00	
805. Lender's Inspection Fee to			
806. Tax Service Fee to Megastar Financial		80.00	
807. Processing Fee to Megastar Financial		250.00	
808. Underwriting Fee to Megastar Financial		350.00	
809. Courier Fee to Megastar Financial		20.00	
810. Flood Cert Fee to Megastar Financial		25.00	
811. Administrative Fee to Megastar Financial		100.00	

Line Items 700 through 811 (Borrower and Seller).

900. ITEMS REQUIRED BY LENDER TO BE PAID IN ADVANCE					
901. Interest From 05/30/03 to 06/01/03 @ $ 23.907600/day (2 days 6.0000%)					47.82
902. Mortgage Insurance Premium months					
903. Hazard Insurance Premium 1.0 years Insurance Co.				POC $480.00	
904.					
905.					
1000. RESERVES DEPOSITED WITH LENDER					
1001. Hazard Insurance	2.000 months @ $	40.00 per month			80.00
1002. Mortgage Insurance	0.000 months @ $	65.00 per month			
1003. City/Town Taxes	months @ $	per month			
1004. County Taxes	2.000 months @ $	200.00 per month			400.00
1005. Assessments	months @ $	per month			
1006.	months @ $	per month			
1007.	months @ $	per month			
1008. Aggregate Adjustment	months @ $	per month			-480.00

Line Items 900 through 1008 (Borrower and Seller).

1100. TITLE CHARGES			
1101. Settlement or Closing Fee	to Northwest Title	125.00	35.00
1102. Abstract or Title Search	to		
1103. Title Examination	to Northwest Title		150.00
1104. Title Insurance Binder	to Northwest Title	50.00	50.00
1105. Document Preparation	to James Scott Stevenson, Attorney		35.00
1106. Notary Fees	to		
1107. Attorney's Fees	to		
(includes above item numbers:	)		
1108. Title Insurance	to Northwest Title as Agent for First American Title Insurance Company	100.00	916.50
(includes above item numbers:	)		
1109. Lender's Coverage	$ 145,440.00	100.00	
1110. Owner's Coverage	$ 161,600.00	916.50	
1111. Courier/Express fee	to Northwest Title	15.00	15.00
1112.	Northwest Title		
1113. 2nd Half 2002 Taxes	to Franklin County Treasurer	1,200.00	

Line Items 1100 through 1113 (Borrower and Seller).

1200. GOVERNMENT RECORDING AND TRANSFER CHARGES

1201. Recording Fees: Deed $ 14.00: Mortgage $ 66.00: Releases $	80.00	
1202. City/County Tax/Stamps: Deed ; Mortgage	0.50	161.60
1203. State Tax/Stamps: Deed ; Mortgage		
1204. County Recorder		
1205. Recordation Fee to Northwest Title	15.00	
1300. ADDITIONAL SETTLEMENT CHARGES		
1301. Survey to ESTIMATE	140.00	
1302. Pest Inspection to ESTIMATE		100.00
1303. Gas Warranty		
1304. Home Warranty to ESTIMATE		385.00
1305.		
1400. TOTAL SETTLEMENT CHARGES (Enter on Lines 103, Section J and 502, Section K)	2,848.32	11,544.10

Line Items 1200 through 1400 (Borrower and Seller).

There is a series of 700 numbers at the top that relate solely to the real estate commissions to be paid on the transaction. You'll see an entry for both the selling and listing agents and the amounts earned. Our example shows these fees charged to the seller. If in the atypical event you have hired your own representation and the seller for whatever reason does not acknowledge them, you could be responsible for their fee. Typically the seller pays these fees.

The remainder of page 2 is similar to the Good Faith Estimate document, itemizing the expenses for the transaction. This example has been completed to complement the previous transaction for clarity. Therefore, some of the fees noted here have no dollar attachment.

For example, Section 1000 for reserves is referring to the escrow account. City taxes and any assessments required for settlement would be noted here. Section 1100 title charges shows no fees for the abstract or title search because there was a title examination.

Section 1300 lists additional settlement charges, such as those paid for a pest inspection, home warranty program, or gas warranty. These warranties may be offered to you as part of the home purchase by the seller, or you may find they are contractually required per the purchase contract. The gas warranty refers to gas line protection, and a home warranty is a policy that covers the mechanics of a home, such as the heating and cooling system. Should there be a repair needed within a specified date of closing, this policy, if used, may offset some of the initial expense to the home buyer. Again, there are regional differences as to what additional settlement charges can be assessed; however, they will all be located on page 2. Finally, line 1400 is the total of the columns to carry over to page 1.

The top third of page 1 is information on the loan type, loan number, and case number (if one has been assigned for either FHA or VA). The buyer, seller, and lender name and address are listed, as well as the place of settlement and date. Most identification numbers are noted at the top of this form. The left side of the form again is for the borrower, the right side for the seller.

Items 101/40l are the final agreed-upon price of the home.

Items 102/402 list any additional items to be sold with the home.

Item 103 is the closing costs from line 1400, page 2 for the borrower.

Items 106 through 112/406 through 412 are if the taxes and any assessments are paid in advance of closing and there needs to be reconciliation.

Items 120/420 are the total of all expenses due by both parties to this point.

Item 201 will reflect any *earnest money* deposits paid on the purchase contract. These moneys are credited back to you, or you may see them returned.

Mortgage Speak _____

Earnest money is good faith money deposited with a third party to reinforce the borrower's intention to purchase.

Item 202 is the mortgage amount you have agreed upon.

Items 203/503 are used for a loan assumption.

Item 502 is the summary of expenses from line 1400 on page 2.

Item 504 is for the seller's existing loan payoff amount.

Item 505 is for if the seller has a second mortgage or home equity loan balance to be paid.

Items 210/510 are any monies set aside for city/town taxes.

Items 211/511 are the reconciliation of taxes. Note that in this example, taxes are a debit on the seller's side and a credit to the borrower because taxes are paid in *arrears*.

Mortgage Speak _____

Arrears is the result of a payment that is rendered after the due date rather than in advance of the due date.

Items 212/512 are for any tax assessments.

Items 220/520 are column totals for gross amount paid by/for borrower and due to seller. Item 220 is the amount you have available from both the lender and the seller to bring to the closing table.

Items 301/601 are the gross amount from/to each party from line 120/420.

Items 302/602 are reiterating the totals from 220/520.

Items 303/603 are final numbers from the borrower and final numbers due to the seller. Item 303 is the money you will need to have for closing after the loan amount has been subtracted.

By reviewing this format alongside your Good Faith Estimate you will begin to understand how the money moves. Once the settlement agent collects the money from the buyer, they are then able to pay the seller their proceeds.

Rather than you writing 20 independent checks at closing, each item is summarized.

Once your final dollar amount is confirmed by all parties, you must be prepared to have "good funds" available for the closing. Money needs to be available as cash and then put into a cashier's check to be presented at the closing. I've seen more than one closing delayed because good funds were not available. As you are moving around money or accumulating money for closing, it's important that it be in the institution that is going to issue you your final check no less than 10 days prior to the closing. Most banks require time to let the funds set, to make certain that they are actually available. We've all deposited checks and had the bank say that there is a hold on the funds for several days. This is the same thing.

And lots of things are coming together for the closing, so it's not unusual for corrections to be made on the day of your closing. Don't get caught up in the frenzy. You can always get your cashier's check for more than the exact amount. The closing agent is always happy to refund you the difference before you leave, and you'll find that it takes some of the stress out of the moment. Also, have the check made payable to yourself. Once you've signed your documents, you can then endorse the check over to the closing company. If, for whatever reason, something were to go wrong at the last minute, your funds are still in your possession.

Bet You Didn't Know

It's no coincidence that if you were to compare your lender Good Faith Estimate with the closing statement, you would notice similarities in the format. There is a standard number-code system that identifies fees and categorizes them according to who pays and what it may be for. The Truth in Lending Disclosure Statement then uses specific sections in its calculation of the APR.

The title company gets instructions from the lender for the closing. The lender will provide a list of the fees it will be charging for the loan process. The settlement agent will also have expenses, for such things as the survey and the recording fees that he or she will add to the lender's expenses. The purchase contract will reveal any additional expenses per the agreement, such as the real estate fees. The title company completes the HUD-1.

Additional Documentation You'll Be Reviewing

The closing agent will usually have a stack of paperwork to review with you. And my experience has been that most of them do a fine job of introducing the document, highlighting its content, and showing where you need to sign and initial. I'll attempt here to introduce you to most of the documents, but each individual lender, and each state for that matter, may have its own specific documents as well.

The note is the legal instrument that obligates you to repay the dollar amount you borrow to the lender.

The mortgage is the document that places a lien, or hold, on your real estate. The property, in effect, is the security to the lender that the note, or money, will be repaid.

A title examination is performed and the courthouse records are checked for present liens or claims against the property. The lender requires the examination as part of the closing process so that they can verify that when they place a lien on the home they're in *first position*, and no one else has a prior claim. The home is their security, after all, should the debt not be repaid.

Mortgage Speak

First position means that the lender has a priority interest in the real property above all others, including the borrower (i.e., having a right to the property as an asset per the terms of the mortgage or deed of trust). Their lien is to be paid off first. Should another vendor/lender wish to stake a claim against the property such as a second mortgage lender, the primary lender's lien should be satisfied before all others. The first position is of critical importance to the lender in the event the borrower were to default on their loan obligation, and the home was to be sold to satisfy that lien.

There are two types of title insurance.

The *Lenders Policy* is issued as protection to the lender that the title examination was accurate and free from defects of title. In most states, the owner's policy is optional and would also protect the homeowner under the same terms. Your title insurance policy today serves the same purpose as your abstract of years past, but is much thinner. An examiner will go to the courthouse and review public records for liens and transfers, but the entire history is not transferred. Attached is an example title commitment for explanation.

The *Title Policy* provides coverage against any claims against the property prior to your taking ownership. You are responsible going forward.

The *Truth in Lending Disclosure Statement* you received at application will now be prepared for the actual date of closing. You will have final information regarding the terms and the APR. It's a good practice to have your application information at hand to compare numbers, so that all questions can be addressed at the closing.

There may be a *Property Survey* for your review and signature. The survey illustrates where the home you're buying or presently live in is situated within the property boundaries. The survey will also show any easements and encroachments that you need to be aware of. Most notably, utility easements that may run along the boundaries of your property are right of ways for the utility company. If you plant a flower bed on an easement, and the utility company needs to dig up a line through their easement, there go your flowers. It's up to the title insurance company to determine if there is anything on the survey that could prohibit clear transfer of title. A garage built over a property line, for example, could be of concern.

There are a variety of disclosures that the state, lender, settlement agent, or realty company may need signed. There may be a disclosure from the title company and/or lender that mentions the procedure if there is a correction that needs to be made on the documents, and how those errors will be handled. There is usually a first-payment-due letter, with information on where and when to send the payment, and the amount. You may also receive information about other services: direct deposit, automatic-payment withdrawal, and bi-weekly payment withdrawal.

The following is a list of a few disclosures you can expect to sign:

- **Name Affidavit:** This verifies that the persons signing the documents are who they say they are. All aliases are also listed. For example, if James A. Doe were to be signing paperwork, they may also have Jimmy Doe, Jamie Doe, James Doe, and J Doe listed on the affidavit to cover all bases.

- **Occupancy Affidavit:** This verifies whether you intend to occupy the property. This is the lender's way of confirming you'll be in the home if they've approved the loan as owner-occupied.

- **Payment Letter:** This disclosure gives you the breakdown of the monthly payment required, and when and where to send the payment.

- **4506:** This document is a government document that, once signed, authorizes the IRS to release to the requestor information on filed tax returns. The lender can request copies for up to 60 days from the date signed to determine if what was received from the borrower is what was filed with the IRS.

Other forms may be standard to your market, so you may ask for specific forms when talking with or gathering information from the real estate board in your area.

> **Bet You Didn't Know**
>
> The lender may have you sign a form to allow them to review the tax returns filed with the IRS. To discourage fraud, the 4506 gives the lender the opportunity to audit information to verify it matched what was provided at loan application. Make certain when you sign the form to limit the time the lender can go back to a maximum of 60 to 90 days from closing. Also, note what items were provided, i.e., the 2002 tax return and 2001 and 2002 W-2s, so as to avoid unnecessary access to personal data.

Holding Title to a Property

In most states, you are given a couple of options on how you wish to be shown as the owner of your property. There are regional differences in documents, but there are a couple of simple guides to consider. Common titles are the following:

- **Individual** refers to a single individual who is taking title alone. Could be described as an individual man/woman or an unmarried man/woman.

- **Joint** refers to ownership with another or others, commonly seen as husband and wife, joint tenants, tenants in common. Some states have other variations on vesting types.

- **Survivorship** refers to the automatic transfer of ownership should one party or another become deceased. Also seen as joint tenant with right of survivorship. This title avoids probate for the property.

The best way to determine which way to hold title would be to talk with your attorney. Because of the complex estate-planning mandates, it's important to have the advice of a legal professional when choosing how you should hold title.

The general warranty deed is the official document used to show the transfer of ownership between seller and buyer. This is one form that only the seller signs at closing, and, once recorded, the borrower usually receives the original back for his or her records.

Tax Considerations with the Closing

Hold on to the settlement statement after closing. It will help you when you begin to prepare for your following year's tax filing. There are a few items that may allow deductions you can take directly from the closing statement with regard to interest, discount points, and taxes.

The advice of a tax professional can often be more valuable than their fee when it comes to how to best utilize a home purchase for tax purposes.

The Least You Need to Know

- Information needed for a loan closing is compiled by the closing agent from many sources and may take time to accumulate.

- There are different closing methods: Round table allows for all parties to meet to sign and escrow affords a separate company the task of reconciling and distributing funds within a window of time.

- Ask for closing documents, including the HUD-1 settlement statement, 24 to 48 hours prior to closing to allow yourself time to formulate questions.

- There are many documents to sign at closing, several of which may have regional specific requirements. It is always best to check with a local representative for up-to-date disclosure requirements.

Chapter 10

Refinancing Your Home

In This Chapter

- Deciding whether to refinance
- Your choices with refinancing your mortgage
- Finding a good refinancing deal
- Using home-equity loans

Falling interest rates typically pique the consumer's awareness of the refinancing process. When rates are drifting downward, it's only normal to want to take advantage of the lower rates and the savings they bring, because, as we know, lower is better. But how is it better? Obviously, if the interest rate is lower, the payment should also be lower. But are there other benefits worth considering when presented with the opportunity to rewrite the mortgage loan? These questions and more are answered in this chapter.

What Is a Refinance?

A loan that is rewritten on the same property, but under different terms, is called a refinance. When a borrower refinances, he or she is, in effect, paying off one mortgage, and replacing it with another. The new loan can be done with the same lending institution, or it can be done with someone else. Regardless, the loan is treated as if it were new, so there are always costs to be paid. There are some services that may be carried over from one mortgage to another, but count on the fees being similar to those of a purchase.

What Can Refinancing Help You Do?

The promise of lower house payments leads most borrowers to seek out the most attractive rates advertised. But we've learned that it's imperative to review the closing costs and interest rates side by side. Be leery of the offers that lure you to consider refinancing "with no money out of your pocket." The age-old saying about looking too good to be true applies well here.

There are many reasons to consider a refinance. The first is to lower your monthly payment. When you're following your budget and a payment goes down, it's a bonus. Money can either be redirected to another bill, or perhaps go into a savings plan. Ask the question "What will you do with that extra cash monthly?" Think about what that money really means to you. Remember, most people think they are refinancing to save money.

So let's assume that the extra money would come in very handy to pay extra toward another monthly obligation. That's good, because in essence you're using those dollars to improve your overall debt ratio. What if you don't have a plan in place for the extra money? Chances are, you'll find that the savings disappear, never to be realized anywhere.

Now, let's assume that the house payment is comfortable, but, like millions of others, you need to take advantage because lower is better. What about refinancing to keep the payment about the same, but perhaps lower the term, or the number of years, you're obligated to pay? Consider going from a 30-year loan to a 20-year loan. Each month you make your payment going forward, a larger portion is being applied to principal. The savings would not be in your pocket exactly, but it's sitting in the equity of your home. It's a plan; you've thought through why you're refinancing, and have used the rate to benefit you in another way.

Perhaps your mortgage can help with debt management. If you have equity built up, then you may be able to tap that savings account to reduce or eliminate other obligations. Or that nest egg could be available for a home-improvement project, the down payment for a second home at your favorite vacation spot, or even college tuition. Mortgages are a desirable way to finance liabilities because of their inherent tax benefit, the interest write-off.

When Is the Best Time to Refinance?

Over the last four years, this question has been one of the most common heard by mortgage lenders around the country. And there is not a quick answer. At a previous place in time, it was thought that unless you could save 2 percent in the interest rate, it was not a good idea to refinance. Times have changed; do not allow yourself to get caught up in the rate game. Rather, evaluate your financial circumstances.

You may find that the rate may help your decision along, but it's the cash flow and your long-term goals that should really guide you in the decision.

When you originally settled on a loan program, you evaluated what your comfort level was. Through that process, you may not have surmised as much, but you made some decisions on long-term objectives. For example, if you chose a 7/1 ARM loan over a 30-year fixed, most likely you had weighed the risks of the adjustments at the end of the eighty-fourth month against the value of the interest rate on the fixed rate loan. In other words, you had decided that either you did not intend to stay in the home longer than seven years, or the rate difference between the 7-year loan and the 30-year loan didn't matter enough to sway you to the conservative side. The lower monthly payment may have also been a deciding factor. Either way, you needed to think through what the home loan was going to accomplish for you long term.

As you contemplate a refinance, the same process will occur again. But this time, you're asking a few other questions. Where are you, at this point in your life financially? Is your debt balanced with your savings, or are you too heavy in debt? Is your savings portfolio diverse? Do you have a fair distribution of assets, for example, money market, CD, real estate? Realize, you're a homeowner now, and with that comes the responsibility of real estate investment. Regardless of whether you have one unit (your home) or 100 units, the value of that asset plays into your investment portfolio.

If you can see the opportunity to either save money monthly or better your cash flow position, and recover your expenses within a reasonable amount of time (it's good to break even at 12 to 18 months; refer to the "Discount Points and the Permanent-Rate Buy-Down" section in Chapter 8), then it's a good time. If you're fulfilling a long-term goal, such as withdrawing equity to reinvest in another asset, then it's okay to refinance.

Otherwise, rethink the refinance.

The Cost to Refinance

When you refinance a property, you are taking out a new loan. And when a new loan is established, expect to pay closing costs again. But it stands to reason that because you already have a loan, some of the expenses should be unnecessary or at the least, offered at a discount.

For example, the lender will typically want a re-evaluation of the home, but rather than a full loan appraisal, you may find that they may only drive by the property and make a visual observation to determine it is in place and its basic condition. Or they may rely on market statistics to verify that the property is in an area where values are increasing rather than decreasing. Both of these reviews are considerably less expensive than a full mortgage loan appraisal. You can expect to save $100 to $200 on a reduced review.

As for the closing fees, if you have your title policy from the previous loan closing, the title agency or escrow company will typically only research the history of the property from the date of the last loan closing through the present, as long as 10 years have not elapsed. By reducing the time to search public records, the cost is reduced and should save you approximately $100 in expenses.

If you can provide your property survey and can state that no structures have been built near or on the property lines, usually another survey can be avoided. A survey is usually $125 to $175.

The closing company should offer to perform the closing at a reduced cost, as a professional courtesy, particularly for a repeat customer. Expect to save $50 to $100 from the original closing.

But some expenses cannot be avoided, such as recording fees, conveyance taxes, and document preparation fees. And it's particularly important to understand the cost of the refinance in relationship to the benefit of the savings. By minimizing the up-front costs of rewriting the loan, the more likely you are to regain your investment within a reasonable time. Be aware of paying for discount points and excess fees, regardless of whether paid at closing or rolled into the loan. The exercise in the "Determining How Much Your Refinance Saves You" section later in this chapter illustrates the concept.

Documentation Needed to Refinance

As with the closing costs and the duplication of information, your lender may be able to get away with abbreviated paperwork for the refinance. For example, both FHA and VA loan programs allow for a "streamline" refinance, that often can avoid the need for an appraisal, income, or asset information. The idea is this: If the overall payment is lower, or less than 20 percent greater than the existing payment, why go back and verify whether the borrower can afford the loan?

A credit report is requested to make certain that the loan is current, but otherwise, no new qualification analysis is done. This is a great way to take advantage of lower rates, without the scrutiny of a requalification.

And to save on closing costs (as mentioned earlier), you will be asked to provide the title policy and property survey from your previous loan closing. It is also helpful if you can give the lender information on your homeowner's insurance policy because the new loan will need to reflect that information.

Bet You Didn't Know

A common VA refinance is the IRRRL (interest rate reduction refinance loan). It requires no appraisal and no verification of income or assets. FHA also offers a Streamlined Refinance, and depending upon the loan circumstances, may or may not require an appraisal and credit qualifying.

Types of Refinances

Refinances are categorized by what purpose the new loan will serve. A *rate/term* refinance denotes that the interest rate or the number of years remaining on the loan will be changing. The borrower, in most cases, is either improving his or her cash flow or trying to build equity faster. Closing costs may be included as part of the balance of the mortgage. This is known as "wrapping fees into the loan" in some parts of the country.

If any additional expenses are added into the loan amount, such as cash-to-payoff debt, then the refinance is considered an *equity take-out*. Regardless of the type of refinance, the lender will want you to keep some of the equity in the home, usually 10–25 percent. There are exceptions to these guides, but remember that when you deviate from the norm, risk and rate typically go up. The property value will be determined through a reappraisal of the home.

It's Your Money

Should you take your equity out of the home through a refinance or a home-equity loan/line of credit? A couple considerations are these: one payment vs. two, payment comparison, risk of payment increase in a line of credit, LTV restrictions, and prepayment of loan vs. amortization over term.

The new loan may also require new verifications of income, assets, and credit. But many lenders offer a streamlined refinance, which may eliminate or significantly reduce additional documentation and qualification. This option may be available if you are changing the rate or term and the payment does not increase dramatically (no greater than 20 percent). No cash may be taken through the loan other than for closing costs.

What's Different About a Refinance Loan?

The basic process of obtaining the mortgage loan will not change. You'll need to decide what the loan is for, and how you would like it structured. The lender will provide payment and cost information that you'll need to compare and evaluate which option suits your long-range goals.

The closing cost considerations are different. When you purchased, the costs were paid up front, by either you or by the seller. When you refinance, you have a choice of paying the expenses or of financing them into the loan. The common way to handle closing costs as part of the loan is to increase the loan balance. Another solution is for the lender to cover the expenses as part of the rate. The par rate is no extra money out of pocket, as discussed in Chapter 8. If that rate goes down, the cost of the money goes up, hence discount points. But as the rate goes up, there is money paid back to the borrower and available to cover closing costs. So when you see a lender advertise no money out of pocket, they're using either the rate or the loan to cover the costs to refinance.

It is a cost to you if the rate goes up because the lender is covering your costs. It is a cost to you if the mortgage balance is increased to cover your refinance. Even if you don't write a check for the costs, they're in the loan somewhere. So for the lender to say no out of pocket, they may be bending the truth.

You'll need to think through whether you want to finance the costs or pay them up front as part of closing. When you refinance, it's as though you've taken a new loan. You'll skip a house payment, leaving you a free month to either cover a portion, if not all, of your refinance expenses, or walk away with the equivalent of your house payment for that month.

If you finance your costs to refinance, you're taking from the house savings, and if you're trying to save money, you've spent money before saving it. By paying for the cost up front, your cash flow remains constant, and you've not used the equity to finance your cost of doing business. An exception is when you're reducing the term of the loan, for example, going from a 30- to a 20- or 15-year term. If you finance your costs, it's not quite so bad because each payment made going forward has a significantly higher principal portion, and you're able to recover the cost of doing the refinance through the additional equity payments.

Determining How Much Your Refinance Saves You

How can you tell if you're saving money with a refinance? A couple of key calculations help you to compare today's loan to a new mortgage. Here is an example, with a table that follows for you to fill in yourself.

Refinance for Rate Reduction	
Today's P&I payment	$1,000.00
New P&I payment	−850.00
Total savings	=150.00
Cost to refinance	2,500.00
Months to recover expense ($2,500.00 ÷ $150.00)	=16.67
Refinance for Cash Out	
Today's P&I payment	$1,000.00
Other debts to be paid off	+525.00
Total expenses	=1,525.00
New P&I payment	−850.00
Savings monthly	675.00
Cost to refinance	2,500.00
Months to recover expense ($2,500.00 ÷ $675.00)	=3.7

Refinance for Rate Reduction

Today's P&I payment	_____
New P&I payment	–_____
Total savings	=_____
Cost to refinance	_____
Months to recover expense	
(_____ ÷ _____)	=_____

Refinance for Cash Out

Today's P&I payment	_____
Other debts to be paid off	+_____
Total expenses	=_____

Refinance for Cash Out

New P&I payment	–_____
Savings monthly	_____
Cost to refinance	_____
Months to recover expense	
(_____ ÷ _____)	=_____

The idea on any refinance is to know why you are refinancing and how the monthly savings will be applied. In the case of a rate/term refinance, the overall interest paid should be reduced, saving you money over the life of the loan. If you choose to do a cash-out refinance to consolidate debt, then you will probably see your overall cash flow improve, saving you money.

Again, "savings" means different things to different households. You only want to refinance if you can foresee the benefit, and recover the expense to do so within 12 to 18 months. Any longer leaves open the question of whether the money spent to refinance will be recovered.

The Home Equity Loan vs. Refinancing

A refinance will cost you money to do, and sometimes that may defeat your purpose. If you're looking for quick, inexpensive cash out of your home, you might explore a home-equity loan or line of credit. The lender will typically do an abbreviated credit/income check and a drive-by appraisal of your home. They'll offer you a loan based upon a percentage of your home value. That maximum loan amount available may vary from lender to lender. You may have more cash available to you by using a home-equity product vs. refinancing because the guides are different.

The rate is based upon the amount of the credit line, your credit score, and how much equity is remaining in the home if the credit line were to be run up to its maximum. There are rarely significant closing costs to obtain the equity loan, which makes them attractive. Because they're easy to obtain, everybody seems to think they need one. Be cautious. As with any available credit, it's for emergencies and not meant to be abused.

The disadvantage to the second mortgage is that there is another payment to contend with, and depending on whether it's fixed or an interest-only revolving loan, the payment movement could be a consideration. It's prudent to compare whether one solution is better than the other.

! Bet You Didn't Know

There is a whole separate process for refinance loans in New York called Extension, Consolidation & Modification Agreements, which is their form of a refinance. Rather than the traditional references we've made here, you will need to find guides specific to New York.

Loan Modification

In rare instances, the lender may allow you to rewrite the loan without refinancing. A loan modification keeps the original terms the same; for example, if it's a 30-year loan at 6.5 percent, the loan will stay as such. But if you have a significant payment toward principal, the lender may be willing to "modify" your payment based upon the new outstanding balance. This process could enable you to take advantage of a lower payment without the expense of refinancing the loan.

Tax Considerations with Refinances

In general, you are permitted to deduct interest paid and property taxes paid in the year they are paid.

When it comes to refinancing, you are often given the option to finance closing costs and pre-paid expenses for taxes and insurance, as value permits. If you elect to do so, you are effectively amortizing the expense of the fees to refinance over the loan's life. In doing so, you may be impacting how much of these expenses can be written off for tax purposes.

And because you are rearranging your payment, expect that the interest you pay yearly will adjust. Having said that, you can also expect that your deductible interest will be modified. It's a good idea to evaluate how this modification will effect you on tax day. Always consult with a tax professional to evaluate the impact.

Conclusion

The purpose of any guide book is information … because information is power. And there is no other way to go but informed when financing a home. There is just too much of your hard-earned savings on the line to proceed any other way. Your home after all is not merely the place you lay your head at night. As we've learned, it is an integral part of your financial makeup. And depending upon your long-term goals, this purchase may be a long-term asset, or one that will be traded within a few years for another.

And by preparing yourself, and understanding the options available, you can assure yourself that the decisions you make will be sound. Align yourself with experts; a lender that can provide good information that you can understand. An informed real estate professional can provide more insight and information than you can compile, assuming they are educated in the market you wish to purchase in. An attorney can offer guidance as well as referrals to professionals within the industry. And a knowledgeable tax advisor can answer all your questions with regard to how this purchase effects you going forward.

Keep in mind when you start the mortgage loan process that it is exactly that—a process. There is a starting point and a yet undetermined end. In the middle is the research and exploration. You've taken a very important step toward the end by reading this book.

The Least You Need to Know

- When refinancing, make certain you understand why and how your are benefiting from the process.

- To refinance means you are rewriting the note, and with that process comes additional fees, some of which have been paid previously when you purchased the home. There may be some credits available.

- There are two major types of refinance: rate/term and cash-out.

- Today there are other ways to obtain the equity or savings from your home. Aside from refinancing, you may also consider opening a second mortgage to access the money in your home.

Appendix

Loan Table

To use this chart, find the interest rate of the loan you are considering in the left column and the term of the loan across the top row. Where that row and column intersect, you will find the monthly payment amount for a $1,000 loan. Then multiple that payment by how many thousands you are borrowing.

For example: A 6 percent loan for 30 years is $6 per month per thousand. If you borrow $150,000, then multiply 150 × $6 to get a $900 payment.

Monthly Payment per $1,000 of Principal Borrowed at Interest Rates from 2 to 19 Percent Over 10- to 30-Year Terms

Rate	10	15	20	25	3F
2.000%	$9.20	$6.44	$5.06	$4.24	$3.70
2.125%	$9.26	$6.49	$5.12	$4.30	$3.76
2.250%	$9.31	$6.55	$5.18	$4.36	$3.82
2.375%	$9.37	$6.61	$5.24	$4.42	$3.89
2.500%	$9.43	$6.67	$5.30	$4.49	$3.95
2.625%	$9.48	$6.73	$5.36	$4.55	$4.02
2.750%	$9.54	$6.79	$5.42	$4.61	$4.08
2.875%	$9.60	$6.85	$5.48	$4.68	$4.15
3.000%	$9.66	$6.91	$5.55	$4.74	$4.22
3.125%	$9.71	$6.97	$5.61	$4.81	$4.28
3.250%	$9.77	$7.03	$5.67	$4.87	$4.35
3.375%	$9.83	$7.09	$5.74	$4.94	$4.42
3.500%	$9.89	$7.15	$5.80	$5.01	$4.49
3.625%	$9.95	$7.21	$5.86	$5.07	$4.56
3.750%	$10.01	$7.27	$5.93	$5.14	$4.63

Rate	10	15	20	25	30
3.875%	$10.07	$7.33	$5.99	$5.21	$4.70
4.000%	$10.12	$7.40	$6.06	$5.28	$4.77
4.125%	$10.18	$7.46	$6.13	$5.35	$4.85
4.250%	$10.24	$7.52	$6.19	$5.42	$4.92
4.375%	$10.30	$7.59	$6.26	$5.49	$4.99
4.500%	$10.36	$7.65	$6.33	$5.56	$5.07
4.625%	$10.42	$7.71	$6.39	$5.63	$5.14
4.750%	$10.48	$7.78	$6.46	$5.70	$5.22
4.875%	$10.55	$7.84	$6.53	$5.77	$5.29
5.000%	$10.61	$7.91	$6.60	$5.85	$5.37
5.125%	$10.67	$7.97	$6.67	$5.92	$5.44
5.250%	$10.73	$8.04	$6.74	$5.99	$5.52
5.375%	$10.79	$8.10	$6.81	$6.07	$5.60
5.500%	$10.85	$8.17	$6.88	$6.14	$5.68
5.625%	$10.91	$8.24	$6.95	$6.22	$5.76
5.750%	$10.98	$8.30	$7.02	$6.29	$5.84
5.875%	$11.04	$8.37	$7.09	$6.37	$5.92
6.000%	$11.10	$8.44	$7.16	$6.44	$6.00

continues

continued

Rate	10	15	20	25	30
6.125%	$11.16	$8.51	$7.24	$6.52	$6.08
6.250%	$11.23	$8.57	$7.31	$6.60	$6.16
6.375%	$11.29	$8.64	$7.38	$6.67	$6.24
6.500%	$11.35	$8.71	$7.46	$6.75	$6.32
6.625%	$11.42	$8.78	$7.53	$6.83	$6.40
6.750%	$11.48	$8.85	$7.60	$6.91	$6.49
6.875%	$11.55	$8.92	$7.68	$6.99	$6.57
7.000%	$11.61	$8.99	$7.75	$7.07	$6.65
7.125%	$11.68	$9.06	$7.83	$7.15	$6.74
7.250%	$11.74	$9.13	$7.90	$7.23	$6.82
7.375%	$11.81	$9.20	$7.98	$7.31	$6.91
7.500%	$11.87	$9.27	$8.06	$7.39	$6.99
7.625%	$11.94	$9.34	$8.13	$7.47	$7.08
7.750%	$12.00	$9.41	$8.21	$7.55	$7.16
7.875%	$12.07	$9.48	$8.29	$7.64	$7.25
8.000%	$12.13	$9.56	$8.36	$7.72	$7.34
8.125%	$12.20	$9.63	$8.44	$7.80	$7.42
8.250%	$12.27	$9.70	$8.52	$7.88	$7.51

Rate	10	15	20	25	30
8.375%	$12.33	$9.77	$8.60	$7.97	$7.60
8.500%	$12.40	$9.85	$8.68	$8.05	$7.69
8.625%	$12.47	$9.92	$8.76	$8.14	$7.78
8.750%	$12.53	$9.99	$8.84	$8.22	$7.87
8.875%	$12.60	$10.07	$8.92	$8.31	$7.96
9.000%	$12.67	$10.14	$9.00	$8.39	$8.05
9.125%	$12.74	$10.22	$9.08	$8.48	$8.14
9.250%	$12.80	$10.29	$9.16	$8.56	$8.23
9.375%	$12.87	$10.37	$9.24	$8.65	$8.32
9.500%	$12.94	$10.44	$9.32	$8.74	$8.41
9.625%	$13.01	$10.52	$9.40	$8.82	$8.50
9.750%	$13.08	$10.59	$9.49	$8.91	$8.59
9.875%	$13.15	$10.67	$9.57	$9.00	$8.68
10.000%	$13.22	$10.75	$9.65	$9.09	$8.78
10.125%	$13.28	$10.82	$9.73	$9.18	$8.87
10.250%	$13.35	$10.90	$9.82	$9.26	$8.96
10.375%	$13.42	$10.98	$9.90	$9.35	$9.05
10.500%	$13.49	$11.05	$9.98	$9.44	$9.15

continues

continued

Rate	10	15	20	25	30
10.625%	$13.56	$11.13	$10.07	$9.53	$9.24
10.750%	$13.63	$11.21	$10.15	$9.62	$9.33
10.875%	$13.70	$11.29	$10.24	$9.71	$9.43
11.000%	$13.78	$11.37	$10.32	$9.80	$9.52
11.125%	$13.85	$11.44	$10.41	$9.89	$9.62
11.250%	$13.92	$11.52	$10.49	$9.98	$9.71
11.375%	$13.99	$11.60	$10.58	$10.07	$9.81
11.500%	$14.06	$11.68	$10.66	$10.16	$9.90
11.625%	$14.13	$11.76	$10.75	$10.26	$10.00
11.750%	$14.20	$11.84	$10.84	$10.35	$10.09
11.875%	$14.27	$11.92	$10.92	$10.44	$10.19
12.000%	$14.35	$12.00	$11.01	$10.53	$10.29
12.125%	$14.42	$12.08	$11.10	$10.62	$10.38
12.250%	$14.49	$12.16	$11.19	$10.72	$10.48
12.375%	$14.56	$12.24	$11.27	$10.81	$10.58
12.500%	$14.64	$12.33	$11.36	$10.90	$10.67
12.625%	$14.71	$12.41	$11.45	$11.00	$10.77
12.750%	$14.78	$12.49	$11.54	$11.09	$10.87

Rate	10	15	20	25	30
12.875%	$14.86	$12.57	$11.63	$11.18	$10.96
13.000%	$14.93	$12.65	$11.72	$11.28	$11.06
13.125%	$15.00	$12.73	$11.80	$11.37	$11.16
13.250%	$15.08	$12.82	$11.89	$11.47	$11.26
13.375%	$15.15	$12.90	$11.98	$11.56	$11.36
13.500%	$15.23	$12.98	$12.07	$11.66	$11.45
13.625%	$15.30	$13.07	$12.16	$11.75	$11.55
13.750%	$15.38	$13.15	$12.25	$11.85	$11.65
13.875%	$15.45	$13.23	$12.34	$11.94	$11.75
14.000%	$15.53	$13.32	$12.44	$12.04	$11.85
14.125%	$15.60	$13.40	$12.53	$12.13	$11.95
14.250%	$15.68	$13.49	$12.62	$12.23	$12.05
14.375%	$15.75	$13.57	$12.71	$12.33	$12.15
14.500%	$15.83	$13.66	$12.80	$12.42	$12.25
14.625%	$15.90	$13.74	$12.89	$12.52	$12.35
14.750%	$15.98	$13.83	$12.98	$12.61	$12.44
14.875%	$16.06	$13.91	$13.08	$12.71	$12.54
15.000%	$16.13	$14.00	$13.17	$12.81	$12.64

continues

continued

Rate	10	15	20	25	30
15.125%	$16.21	$14.08	$13.26	$12.91	$12.74
15.250%	$16.29	$14.17	$13.35	$13.00	$12.84
15.375%	$16.36	$14.25	$13.45	$13.10	$12.94
15.500%	$16.44	$14.34	$13.54	$13.20	$13.05
15.625%	$16.52	$14.43	$13.63	$13.30	$13.15
15.750%	$16.60	$14.51	$13.73	$13.39	$13.25
15.875%	$16.67	$14.60	$13.82	$13.49	$13.35
16.000%	$16.75	$14.69	$13.91	$13.59	$13.45
16.125%	$16.83	$14.77	$14.01	$13.69	$13.55
16.250%	$16.91	$14.86	$14.10	$13.79	$13.65
16.375%	$16.99	$14.95	$14.19	$13.88	$13.75
16.500%	$17.06	$15.04	$14.29	$13.98	$13.85
16.625%	$17.14	$15.13	$14.38	$14.08	$13.95
16.750%	$17.22	$15.21	$14.48	$14.18	$14.05
16.875%	$17.30	$15.30	$14.57	$14.28	$14.16
17.000%	$17.38	$15.39	$14.67	$14.38	$14.26

Index